Alpha to Ωmega

Stage One Plus Activity Pack

Bevé Hornsby and Julie Pool
in collaboration with Neysa Moss

Heinemann

Heinemann Educational Publishers
Halley Court, Jordan Hill, Oxford OX2 8EJ
A division of Reed Educational and Professional Publishing Ltd

Heinemann is a registered trademark of Reed Educational and Professional Publishing Limited

OXFORD MADRID ATHENS FLORENCE PRAGUE CHICAGO PORTSMOUTH NH (USA)
MEXICO CITY SÃO PAULO SINGAPORE KUALA LUMPUR TOKYO MELBOURNE
AUCKLAND NAIROBI KAMPALA IBADAN GABORONE JOHANNESBURG

© Bevé Hornsby and Julie Pool 1997
First published 1997

ISBN 0 435 10420 9

2001 2000 99 98 97
10 9 8 7 6 5 4 3 2 1

The worksheets may be reproduced by individual teachers without permission from the publisher. All other material remains © Heinemann Educational Books and may not be reproduced in any form for any purpose without the prior permission of Heinemann Educational Books.

Designed and typeset by Artistix, Thame, Oxon
Cover design by Aricot Vert
Printed in Great Britain by Athenaeum Press Ltd, Gateshead, Tyne and Wear
Bound in Edinburgh by Hunter & Fouls Ltd

DEDICATION

To Bevé's husband, Arthur Buckham, and Julie's brothers, Armin and Ray Bendiner, who all passed away while this book was being written

ACKNOWLEDGEMENTS

We are deeply indebted to Neysa Moss and Patricia Fell who have written many pages in this book. Without their efforts, this book would never have been written. Our thanks also to Janice Whitten, our publisher at Heinemann Educational and our editor Rachel Normington, who have been very understanding and helpful when times have been particularly difficult.

The Authors and Publishers should like to thank the following for permission to use copyright material:

Jennifer Luithlen Agency for the Tongue Twisters on page 14, from *The World's Toughest Tongue Twisters* by Joseph Rosenblum; 'Going through the old photos' (p58 26 lines) by Michael Rosen from *You Tell Me: Poems* by Roger McGough and Michael Rosen (Kestrel Books, 1979) copyright © Michael Rosen, 1979. Reproduced by permission of Frederick Warne & Co., pp82, 83; Random House Inc for *Treasure Island* and *Kidnapped* by Robert Louis Stevenson, adapted by Lisa Norby from the Bullseye Series and for *Oliver Twist* by Charles Dickens, adapted by Les Martin from the Bullseye Series, pp85–9; Heinemann Educational Publishers for adapted text from *Living in the 1940s* and *We were there The 1940s* by Rosemary Rees & Judith Maguire, pp93, 94; Hutton Getty/Getty Images Ltd, p93.

The Publishers have made every effort to trace the copyright holders, but if they have inadvertently overlooked any, they will be pleased to make the necessary arrangements at the first opportunity.

Contents

Alpha to Omega References (4th Edition)	Contents	Sheet Number
	Introduction	v
	Teacher's notes	vi
23	Open syllable words flashcards	1
23	Open syllable practice	2
22–24	Vowels snap	3–4
24	Short vowels: tracking and fill 'em ups	5
24	Short vowel tracking	6
24	Short vowel fill 'em ups	7
24	Short vowels families game	8
30	'f'/'v'/'th' list 1	9
30	Student marking grid	10
30	'f'/'v'/'th' list 2 – Mixed	11
30	Student marking grid	12
30	'f'/'v'/'th' picture fill 'em ups	13
30	Tongue twisters ('f' and 'th')	14
28	Initial blends	15
28	More smashing initial blends	16
28	Tracking for triple blends	17
35	Assimilation	18
30–36	Finding the final blends	19
30–36	Final blends and assimilations – Mix and match	20
28–36	The battle of the blends balloons 1–3	21–23
42–43	'ed' list	24
42–43	Student marking grid	25
42–43	'ed' endings 1–2	26–27
42–43	'ed' proofreading	28
45, 50, 55	Word sums	29
48	'er' 'ur' 'ir' have the same sound	30
48	'er' 'ur' 'ir' fill 'em ups	31
48	Top of the tower	32–33
52–56	Wave the witch's wand	34
52–56	Wave the wand game	35–36
58–71	The flossy families game	37–39
58	'll' tracking and cloze poem	40
64	'ss' tracking and cloze poem	41
69	'ff' tracking and cloze poem	42
71	'ck' tracking and cloze poem	43
58–70	Flossy words multiple choice	44
58–70	An odd flossy ode	45
92	Soft 'c'	46
92–97	'c' or 'k'	47
92–97	Camping or not – 'c', 'k' or 'ck'	48
92–97	Mar_'s _rossword	49

Alpha to Omega Activity Pack One Plus

Contents

99–102	Gentle soft 'g'	50
99–102	Tracking for 'g': saying /g/ or /j/	51
99–102	Fill the golden jar with gems	52
91	'o' saying /u/	53
106	'u' as a wall proofreading	54
107	'd' as a wall to keep the vowel short	55–56
108	't' as a wall for no reason at all!	57–58
76–87	a e i o u are vowels	59
76–87	Long and short vowel fill 'em ups	60
148	Double or not	61–63
76–87	Magic 'e'	64
76–87	Long vowel families game	65
151	Drop the silent 'e'	66–67
151	Double, drop or not	68
109	Long vowel sound – short vowel spelling word search	69
31–109	Odd words	70
	Past tense, present tense, future tense	71
	Verbs	72–73
	Nouns	74–75
	Apostrophe	76
	Questions?	77
	Yes or no questions	78
	Intonation	79
	Busy, dizzy commas	80
	Commas and speech marks	81
	Ready for rhyming	82–83
	Sequencing: How to cook spaghetti	84
	Sentence sequencing – *Treasure Island*	85
	Paragraph sequencing – *Kidnapped*	86
	Comprehension – *Oliver Twist*	87–92
	Comprehension – A wedding day in the 1940s	93–95
	Words you need to know 1: Exam words – Mix and match	96
	Words you need to know 2: Exam words – Cloze passage	97
	Words you need to know 3: Exam words – Crossword puzzle	98
	Words you need to know 4: English – Mix and match	99
	Words you need to know 5: English – Crossword puzzle	100
	Words you need to know 6: Maths – Mix and match	101
	Words you need to know 7: Maths – Crossword puzzle	102
	Words you need to know 8: General science – Mix and match	103
	Words you need to know 9: General science – Crossword puzzle	104
	Words you need to know 10: Biology – Mix and match	105
	Words you need to know 11: Biology – Crossword puzzle	106
	Words you need to know 12: Chemistry – Mix and match	107
	Words you need to know 13: Chemistry – Crossword puzzle	108
	Words you need to know 14: Physics – Mix and match	109
	Words you need to know 15: Physics – Crossword puzzle	110

Alpha to Omega Activity Pack One Plus

Introduction

This pack has been written in response to many requests to provide a bridge between *Alpha to Omega Activity Pack Stage 1* and *Alpha to Omega Activity Pack Stage 2*. It is aimed primarily at students aged 10+ who have some reading skills but are still struggling with spelling and reading comprehension. The pack covers remediation of phonic skills and also provides practice with basic language and grammatical structures. The reading level is *Stage 2* of *Alpha to Omega* while the spelling exercises do not go beyond *Stage 1*.

▶ **Phonological acquisition** is revised with particular practice in the more difficult initial and final consonant blends. For example, difficult areas like /f/, /v/ and /th/ can be consolidated using the exercises provided, following on from *Stage 1*.

▶ **Spelling patterns** using walls (/d/, /u/, /t/) are also covered and there is useful reinforcement of /w/ and of /k/, /c/ and /ck/ which are not covered again in *Stage 2*.

▶ **Short vowel sounds** and their names are established in *Stage 1* and exercises and games provided in this pack will encourage automaticity.

▶ **The 'magic e' rule for long vowel sounds** is covered in *Stage 1* and the long vowel sound with short vowel spelling is practised in this section; thus providing a bridge to the long vowel digraphs in *Stage 2*.

▶ More practice of **vowel consonant digraphs** is provided. *Stage 1* covers /er/, /or/ and /ar/ as well as /er/, /ur/ and /ir/ which are given exercises here.

▶ **Early stages of suffixing** are included, such as adding 'ed' and 'ing' as these are needed in the early stages of story writing.

▶ **Grammatical structures** covered in *Stage 2* are practised at a simpler level.

▶ **Comprehension questions** are designed to reinforce work carried out in schools at Key Stage 2 and to help students move into Key Stage 3.

▶ **Subject vocabulary exercises** are designed to help students to become familiar with vocabulary that they will meet at Key Stage 3.

We do hope you and your students enjoy using the games, activities and exercises in *Alpha to Omega Activity Pack One Plus*.

Teacher's Notes

General Advice. The rules and directions given for games and exercises are flexible. Please feel free to re-interpret, cut out or otherwise adapt them to your needs and those of your students.

1 **Open syllable words flashcards.** This sheet is for those who are just learning to read and spell. Although some are irregular, such as 'the', 'to', 'do', 'by' and 'my', these words are vital to learn at the very first stages of reading and spelling. The sheet should be photocopied on to a sheet of label paper and stuck on card. It can then be cut up and used as flashcards.

2 **Open syllable practice.** All of the words to be found in the tracking are at the top of the page. Tracking should be done from left to right. It is important to check for backtracking which should not happen if the pupil is tracking carefully. Only the words at the top are required to complete the Fill 'em Ups.

3, 4 **Vowels snap.** This is a game of practice both for the terms used for vowels and of the vowels themselves. It can be played by a student on his or her own or in a group. The purpose is automaticity, i.e. that the student knows internally and immediately that a long vowel says its name and a short vowel says its sound.

To make the game up, photocopy the sheets on to sticky-backed label paper. Cut the labels up to stick on card. Each vowel has its own card. 'Long' and 'name' go on opposite sides of the same card; 'short' and 'sound' go on opposite sides of the same card.

The cards should be mixed and divided into two piles: vowels and terms. The terms cards should be mixed back to front as well as amongst themselves.

A player on his or her own should turn over a card from each pile simultaneously and say out loud the sound which is represented, e.g. long a, short o, name e, sound i. In the beginning, it should be played slowly and checked for accuracy, but, with time and practice, it can be timed as a speed game.

In a game for two, one player holds the vowels and the other holds the terms. They place the cards on the table simultaneously and the student who says the requested sound first wins the cards. The player with the most cards wins.

In a team game, this can be used to see which team completes their cards first and most accurately.

These cards can also be used for learning short or long vowels on their own.

5 **Short vowels: tracking and fill 'em ups.** This sheet offers basic practice in finding the short vowel sounds through tracking. The directions suggest that each short vowel sound be tracked separately and in the order of most frequent confusion for the learners. The fill 'em ups offer more practice in mixed identification of the short vowel sounds.

6 **Short vowel tracking.** This sheet is the first part of a two-part story. The purpose of the exercise is for the student to find the short vowel sounds in the words; however, the reading level is quite high so the story may need to be read to the students.

7 **Short vowel fill 'em ups.** This sheet is the second part of the story. Again, the reading level is quite high, so it might be useful to read the story to your students first. Then they should fill in the missing letters.

8 **Short vowels families game.** This game can be played separately or mixed together with the Long Vowels Families Game (**65**) depending on time and teacher. Both games can also be played with a group or with only two players. The object of each game is the same: to gather as many families as possible – that is, all five cards with the same long or short vowel sound. The vowel sound is printed at the top of each card. There are five short vowel sound families and five long vowel sound families.

Alpha to Omega Activity Pack One Plus

Teacher's Notes vii

Two players (frequently student/teacher): Give a different sound card to each player, keeping aside one card from the other three families. Put the other cards in a pile, printed side down. The student turns over a card, reads the sound and then the word in bold. If read correctly and it matches his/her family card, he/she keeps it. Otherwise, it goes to the bottom of the pile. The teacher then does the same. As soon as a complete family is gathered, the group is put on the table, face up, and the player gets another card with a new sound family. The player with the most completed families wins.

More than two players: Each player is dealt four cards. First, each player sorts out his/her cards and puts together those with the same sound (the same family). The first player asks the player on his/her left for a card s/he needs to complete a family (or families) in his/her hand. If another player has a requested card, s/he asks again until there are no more to be given. It is now the second player's turn to ask the player on her/his left for cards to complete her/his family. The game continues until all the families are complete. The player with the most completed families win.

9–12 **'f'/'v'/'th' discrimination lists.** This exercise consists of three lists of words (9) with 'f', 'v' and 'th' in the initial, medial and final positions and another list (11) of mixed words; two student marking grids are provided. The student(s) should repeat the words so that they can **feel** as well as hear the differences between 'f', 'v' and 'th'. The student(s) should then mark on the marking grid which sound they hear and feel for each word.

13 **'f'/'v'/'th' picture fill 'em ups.** The student is asked to complete the words by writing in 'f', 'v' or 'th' to make the word match the picture.

14 **Tongue twisters – 'f' and 'th'.** These are fun exercises to help students to practise the differentiation between 'f' and 'th'.

15 **Initial blends.** The student should read the words and underline the initial blends. They are then asked to complete the words to make them match the pictures.

16 **More smashing initial blends.** The student should read the words and colour in the blends. They should then complete the words to match the pictures.

17 **Tracking for triple blends.** This is a tracking sheet for seeing, hearing and feeling the triple blends. The outline letters should be coloured as the sound is said.

18 **Assimilation.** This sheet contains two exercises: a cloze poem and a multiple choice exercise.

19 **Finding the final blends.** This is a tracking exercise in which the student is asked to read the words and circle the final blends.

20 **Final blends and assimilations mix and match.** In this exercise the student is asked to make real words from the beginnings and endings provided.

21–23 **The battle of the blends balloons.** This is a board game for two or more players. It includes a handicap to make the game more challenging for the teacher. The directions are included on the sheet with the forfeit cards. The board covers two pages which should be copied and joined together so the trail forms a 'B'. Use a die showing ones and twos only.

Alpha to Omega Activity Pack One Plus

viii Teacher's Notes

24, 25 **'ed' discrimination list.** This is another list of words which should be read to the student(s) to help them to hear the three sounds made by 'ed'. It is important to emphasise to them that they are marking the sound they hear – not the spelling, which is always 'ed' with these words. The exercise which follows uses the same words, but the students are now asked to write in 'ed'.

26, 27 **'ed' endings.** This is the same list of words as were heard in the previous exercise. The students are now expected to write in 'ed'. Underneath each word is the sound heard. Therefore, the two exercises together become self-marking.

28 **'ed' proofreading.** This is another proofreading in story form. The student(s) should read the story and correct the mistakes.

29 **Word sums.** This is an exercise both to teach word sums and to reinforce time-telling. The student(s) is given a time on an analogue clock to find two syllables which fit together to make a word.

Answers:
1 border
2 carpet
3 market
4 permit
5 garden
6 partly

30 **'er', 'ur', 'ir' have the same sound.** The student(s) should read the words and colour in the 'r' digraphs. They should then write in the word from the list to match the picture.

31 **'er', 'ur', 'ir' fill 'em ups.** The student(s) should choose the correct spelling and underline or highlight it. They should then write the sentences out, correctly spelled, on the lines provided.

32, 33 **Top of the tower.** This a challenging game of completion. The students are asked to fill in the 'r' digraph necessary to complete the words. It would be sensible to copy not only the game on to label paper but also the cards and to cover the cards in film so that they can be reused.

34 **Wave the witch's wand.** The student(s) should first read the first sentence to **hear** the change in sound. They should then use coloured pens to fill in the different sounds. In the last exercise, they are asked to select the correct spelling for the word and write it in the space provided.

35, 36 **Wave the wand.** This game reinforces the 'w' rules and is for two or more players. The rules are as follows:

Place the counters on the starting line. Shuffle the cards and place them in a pile, face down. The first player turns over a card and reads the word. If a 'w' word is read correctly, the player moves forward **two** squares. If one of the other words is read correctly, the player moves **one** square. The teacher always moves **one** square. The first player to reach the finish line wins.

The word cards are on the following sheet.

37–39 **The flossy families game.** There are four families containing six cards each: five word cards and a rule card. The object of the game is to acquire as many complete families as possible. The game may be played by two to four players. The cards are shuffled and all are distributed. Each player should sort his/her cards into families. Then each takes turns to complete as many families as possible by asking for a word which s/he does not have. The player with the most families wins.

Alpha to Omega Activity Pack One Plus

Teacher's Notes

40 **'ll' tracking and cloze poem.** This is the first in a series of cloze poem exercises. There is always a tracking first, or a choice. The students should track the words first, reading them and colouring in the double letters. Then they should read and try to work out the poem. Sometimes the rhymes are rather obscure and it may be necessary to refer to the answers.

Answers:

'll' cloze poem

This is a poem about nothing at **all**.

Just be careful that you don't **fall**.

You might get a **thrill**

Cycling fast down**hill**

Or you might feel very **small**

When you ride into a **wall**.

Your teacher might say that you know how to **spell**

All of those words that end in '**ll**',

So to all of you who have done so **well**,

Congratulations. I think you're **swell**.

41 **'ss' tracking and cloze poem.** As for 'll' words.

Answers:

'ss' cloze poem

Bess is the **boss**

And she gets **cross**.

She makes a great **fuss**

When we get on the **bus**.

At school, she comes into the **class**

And says she will **pass**.

I really must **stress**

That this lass is a **mess**.

Throw her a **kiss**

and all will be **bliss**.

42 **'ff' tracking and cloze poem.** As for 'll' words.

Answers:

'ff' cloze poem

The **giraffe**

had a laugh

As he clung to the **cliff**,

With his neck very **stiff**,

He took a deep **sniff**.

"What, on earth,

is that smelly **stuff**?

It isn't **coffee**,

It can't be **toffee**.

What, oh what, can this be?

I'd better be **off**

Before I cough

Not another **puff**

Of that awful **stuff**".

43 **'ck' tracking and cloze poem.** As for 'll' words.

Answers:

'ck' cloze poem

It's time to take **stock**

of the time on the **clock**.

We won't have much **luck**

If we really get **stuck**.

We can pack and be **quick**

Take clothes that are **thick**.

You're on a good **wicket**

If you stick with this **ticket**.

Alpha to Omega Activity Pack One Plus

Teacher's Notes

44 **Flossy words multiple choice.** This is a chance for the student to show off their knowledge. S/he chooses the correct spelling. It might be a good idea after this exercise is completed to ask the student(s) to copy the correct sentences into their exercise books or on to their own paper.

45 **An odd flossy ode.** This is the culmination of the rhyming exercise. The rules are mixed. These poems are meant mainly for enjoyment and not to be taken too seriously. If the students have difficulties, please help them. Polysyllabic words have been used in some poems for rhyming purposes and sense.

Answers:

An odd flossy ode

To get this far, you have done very **well**

To complete the silly poems I **tell**.

You may have had a bit of **luck**

But some of you, I'm sure, got **stuck**.

The flossy words take a bit of **skill**

Which I know you have and always **will**.

Keep up the practice and don't make a **mess**

Think of the teachers that you will **impress**.

Finished is the huff and **puff**

And I must go and call your **bluff**.

46 **Soft 'c'.** The words in the list should be read aloud. The open letters should be highlighted or coloured in different colours. In the tracking at the bottom, two different coloured pens should be used, preferably red and blue, with the colour coordinated with the spelling. The colours should then be used to highlight the spellings in the tracking.

47 **'c' or 'k' – that was a nice kick.** After learning the rule, the student is asked to write in the 'c' or 'k' to complete the word and, therefore, the sentence. The completed sentence should then be read and written on the line(s) provided.

48 **Camping or not – 'c', 'k' or 'ck'.** In the multiple choice sentences, the students are asked to underline the correct spellings. They should then highlight the spelling pattern. It would be useful for them to write the sentences out correctly in their exercise books or on paper. The following exercise is a proofreading in which they are asked to correct the spelling errors and copy the corrected version. The two exercises together create a story.

49 **Mar_'s _rossword.** This puzzle follows up the theme of 'c', 'k' and 'ck'. The clues across are mostly definitions, while the clues down are mainly sentence completion. One word does not fit the pattern at all, so beware.

Answers:

								¹b		
					²c	³k	i	s	⁴s	
					i			c	⁵i	c	e
				⁶c	e	n	t	u	r	y		t		
			⁷k	i	d		y			c		⁸c
⁹k			r							l		i
i				¹⁰c	o	¹¹k		¹²c	e	n	t	r	e
¹³c	a	l	l			i		i				c
k			e			c		r				u
						¹⁴k	i	c	k	s		s
								l				
				¹⁵k	i	t	e					

Alpha to Omega Activity Pack One Plus

Teacher's Notes

50 **Gentle soft 'g'.** The students are asked to read the words and colour in the spelling patterns. There follows a mnemonic for remembering the exceptions and a matching exercise.

51 **Tracking for 'g' saying /g/ or /j/.** The student is asked to choose two colours, one to highlight the /j/ sound and the other to highlight the /g/ sound. They are forewarned to be wary of the exceptions that are included in the tracking. In the following exercise they are asked to complete the words and write the corrected sentence on the lines provided.

52 **Fill the golden jar with gems.** The cards should be cut up and shuffled. The instructions for playing are included on the sheet.

53 **'o' saying /u/.** The words at the top of this sheet should be used for tracking. The 'o's making the /u/ sound should be coloured. The words from the tracking should then be written into the sentences below to make them complete. The completed sentences should then be written into an exercise book or on paper.

54 **'u' as a wall proofreading.** Read the passage and correct the mis-spellings. Copy the paragraph on to the lines provided.

55 **'d' as a wall to keep the vowel short – fill 'em ups and proofreading.** Fill in the missing letters to complete the words. All the words are provided above. The proofreading should be read, corrected and copied into an exercise book or on to some paper.

56 **'d' as a wall multiple choice poem.** To complete the poem, the student should choose the correct spelling of the missing word and write it in the space provided.

57 **'t' as a wall fill 'em ups poem.** It may be easier with this poem to fill in the missing words before reading it. Otherwise I would suggest that the teacher read it to the student(s) with the blanks filled in before the students fill it in themselves.

58 **'t' as a wall proofreading.** The student(s) should read and correct the story. They should then copy it on to the lines provided.

59 **a e i o u are vowels.** This sheet presents a visual mnemonic for short and long vowel sounds as well as representing the macron and the breve.

60 **Long and short vowel fill 'em ups.** The student is asked to choose the correct spelling and write it in the space provided.

61–63 **Double or not.** This series of exercises is introduced by a teaching page showing the pattern of change in one-syllable words containing a short vowel when a suffix is added which starts with a vowel. Sheet 61 should be cut up so that the student can place the cards over the letters of c v̆ c words which they have written or made with cards and see the doubling pattern. The following sheets are practice sheets: the first sheet contains two tables, one with words in which doubling is required and one in which it is not. Sheet 63 contains a table of mixed doubling and non-doubling words. There is a brief Fill 'em ups exercise at the end to give practice in context.

Alpha to Omega Activity Pack One Plus

Teacher's Notes

64 Magic 'e'. The student(s) should read the words and place them in the appropriate columns below.

65 Long vowels families game. See **Short vowels families game**.

66–67 Drop the silent 'e'. Teaching sheet and exercises similar to **Double or not**.

68 Double, drop or not. Exercises similar to **Double or not**. A short proofreading exercise follows.

69 Long vowel sound – short vowel spelling word search. This is a wordsearch of words with a short vowel spelling but a long vowel sound. It goes from left to right and top to bottom. All the words above the puzzle are hidden in the puzzle. None of them is intentionally repeated except for those found within other words.

Answers:

70 Odd words puzzle. All of the words to be found in the puzzle are listed above. When the puzzle is correctly completed, the letters in the bold squares going down will tell the student just how good s/he is. This makes the puzzle self-marking.

Alpha to Omega Activity Pack One Plus

Teacher's Notes   xiii

71 **Past tense – present tense – future tense.** This is an exercise with verbs and time. It is an essential part of learning and one where there is great difficulty. Students need as much practice as possible.

72–73 **Verbs.** These sheets give practice in changing the tense of verbs. It might be useful to use the time line on the previous sheet to help the student(s) internalise a sense of time.

74 **Nouns.** The first part of this page is an exercise in the use of articles. The student is asked to read the story and fill in the missing indefinite articles. The second part of the sheet deals with plural nouns. Some of them are regular, but most of them are not.

75 **Proper and common nouns; pronouns.** This page contains two exercises: one on proper and common nouns and the other on pronouns. In the first exercise the student is asked to choose two colours and underline the proper nouns with one colour while using the other colour to circle the common nouns. In the exercise on pronouns the student is asked to replace the proper nouns with pronouns and write the sentence out correctly.

76 **Apostrophe.** This sheet revises both uses of the apostrophe: possessive and short form. The first exercise asks for replacement of the apostrophe while the second asks for the apostrophe to be inserted.

77 **Questions.** The first exercise on this page asks the student to identify the word which turns each sentence into a question. The second exercise asks the student to insert the word to create a question.

78 **Yes or no questions.** The first exercise asks the student to change the statement into a yes or no question. The second exercise asks the student to reverse the procedure and make a question into a statement.

79 **Intonation.** This exercise asks the student to listen to the inflection used in asking questions. The introductory questions should be read aloud with emphasis. The student should then write out the next question three times, each time underlining the word s/he has emphasised. The student is then asked to create her/his own question which can be inflected in a variety of ways.

80 **Busy, dizzy commas.** This is an exercise reinforcing commas used in lists. The student is asked to read the poem. Then s/he should choose three colours and underline the nouns in the first verse, the verbs in the second verse and the adjectives in the third verse. S/he should then put the commas in where they belong.

81 **Commas and speech marks.** This is an exercise for reinforcing the uses of commas with speech marks. The student is asked to read the story and fill in the missing commas and speech marks.

82–83 **Ready for rhyming.** The student should read the first poem. S/he should underline the words which rhyme. On sheet 83 the poem is printed again, but the rhyming words are missing. This sheet should be completed with as little return as possible to the complete poem.

84 **Sequencing: how to cook spaghetti.** This is a series of five pictures which should be put in order. They should be photocopied on to label paper, cut out and stuck on card to last longer. Sentences to match the pictures have also been provided. For durability, these too should be cut out and stuck on card. The student should order the pictures and, if requested and capable, match the sentences to the pictures.

85 **Sentence sequencing.** This is a passage from *Treasure Island*. The student is asked to put the sentences in order and to write the sentences out in the correct order on the lines provided. This exercise may be cut up, if desired.

Alpha to Omega Activity Pack One Plus

Teacher's Notes

[86] Paragraph sequencing. This is an excerpt from *Kidnapped*. The student is asked to cut out the paragraphs and put them in order.

Answer:

But at that moment, the tide caught the *Covenant*. The ship spun around like a top. It crashed into a reef with such force that I was knocked off my feet. Seconds later, a huge wave tilted the ship onto her side, and I was thrown into the sea.

I went down twice. When I came up for the second time, the current had swept me far from the *Covenant*. I grabbed hold of a piece of floating timber and began kicking my way toward the shore.

An hour later, I was cast up onto a small island. I had swallowed a good bit of the sea. My legs felt like logs. But I dared not lie down to rest. It was a cold night. In my wet clothes I was in danger of freezing to death. So I walked the shore until dawn.

My little island was separated from the larger Isle of Mull by a deep creek. Across the water I could see the smoke from a chimney. But I was no swimmer.

For three days I slept in a crude shelter. Small shellfish clung to the rocks along the shore. I picked them off and ate them raw. I was so hungry that they tasted wonderful.

On the fourth day I saw two fishermen in a boat. I screamed for help. Instead of coming to rescue me, they laughed. One of them shouted at me. I could hardly hear him, but I made out the word "tide".

All at once I understood. I had been roaming the island for four days, but every time I came to the creek it was high tide. Now I waited for the tide to go out. Nothing was left of the creek but a trickle of water. I walked across to the Isle of Mull.

[87–92] Comprehension: Oliver Twist. This comprehension is based on those done in the SATs at Key Stage Two. It includes the written sections about the characters, the story and the student's opinion of the story.

[93–95] Comprehension: A wedding day in the 1940s. This non-fiction comprehension is based on history and experience. It is intended to lead up to those done at Key Stage Three and includes a vocabulary exercise.

[96–110] Words you need to know

[96] Exam words mix and match. This exercise is to help students to understand the vocabulary used in exam questions. The student should learn the word meanings. It is best if the sheet is cut up and the words and meanings put on separate cards. They can then be mixed up and matched.

[97] Exam words cloze passage. In this exercise the student is asked to write the appropriate words from sheet 96 in the spaces given. The definitions are given in brackets. The exercise is based on the comprehension exercise, 'A wedding day in the 1940s'.

Answers:

Comment on how the **layout** helps you to understand the problems people had getting married during the Second World War.

Describe Kitty's job during the war. What does the **phrase** 'decode messages' in the **passage** mean? Give your **reasons** to **support** what you have written.

Refer to the passage about Kitty and Frank and **explain** why Kitty had to delay their wedding.

Imagine that you are Frank. How would you **persuade** your mother that Kitty really wants to marry you?

Alpha to Omega Activity Pack One Plus

Teacher's Notes   XV

98   **Exam words crossword puzzle.** A challenge for your students.

Answer:

						¹c					
	²p					o			³r		
	e				⁴i	m	a	g	i	n	e
	r					m			a		
⁵d	e	s	c	r	i	b	e		s		
	u					n	⁶l	a	y	o	u	t
	a					t			n		
⁷s		d			⁸p				s		
u	⁹e	x	p	l	a	i	n				
p					s						
¹⁰p	h	r	a	s	e	s					
o					a						
¹¹r	e	f	e	r		g					
t						e					

99   **English words mix and match.** Same as **Exam words mix and match**.

100   **English words crossword puzzle.** Same as **Exam words crossword puzzle**.

Answer:

¹p	²a	r	a	g	r	a	p	h	
	d								
	v		³s						
	e		e						
⁴p	r	o	n	o	u	n		⁵p	
	b		t					h	
			e			⁶v	e	r	b
⁷n	o	u	n					a	
			c					s	
⁸a	d	j	e	c	t	i	v	e	

Alpha to Omega Activity Pack One Plus

xvi Teacher's Notes

101 **Maths words mix and match.** Same as **Exam words mix and match**.

102 **Maths words crossword puzzle.** Same as **Exam words crossword puzzle**.

Answer:

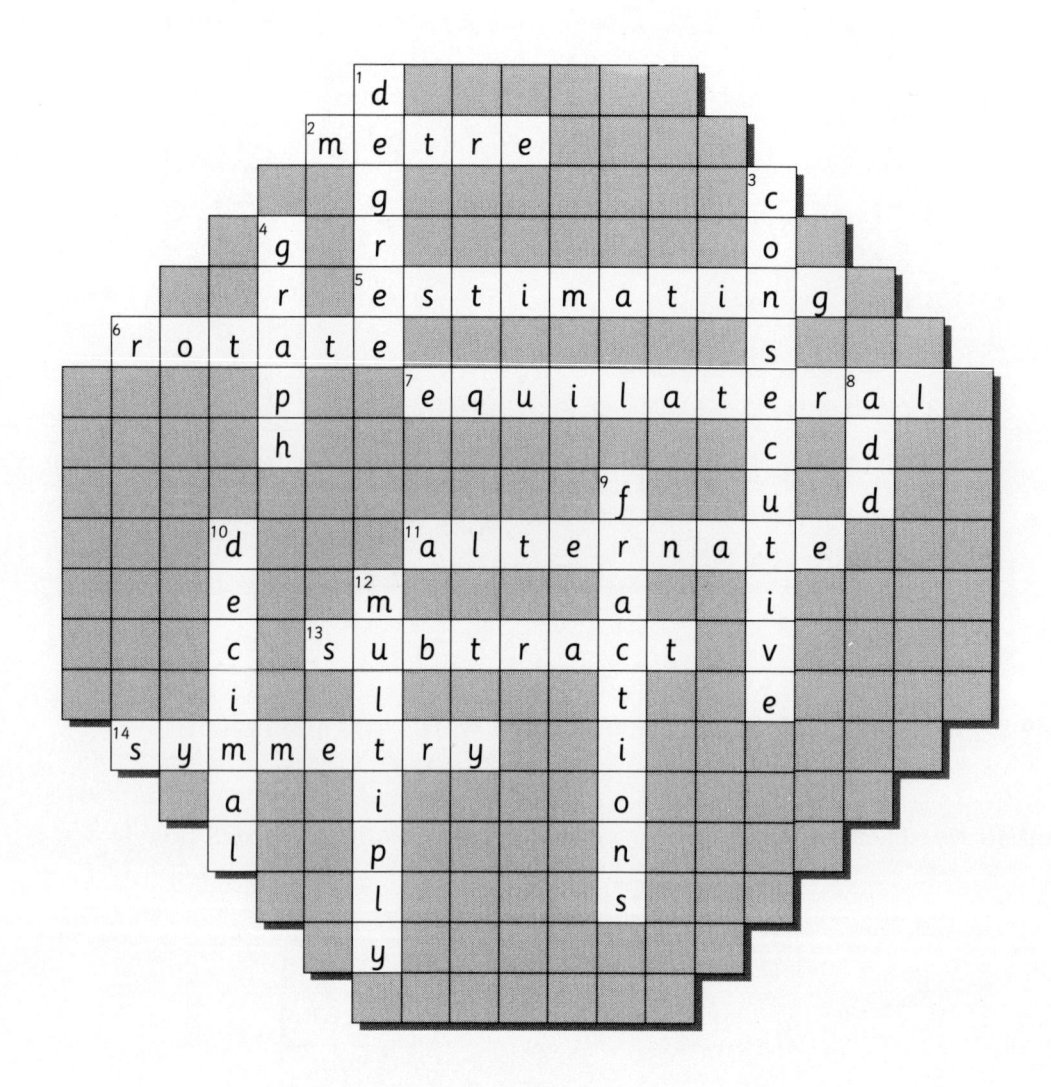

				¹d						
			²m	e	t	r	e			
				g					³c	
		⁴g		r					o	
			r	⁵e	s	t	i	m	a	t	i	n	g
⁶r	o	t	a	t	e				s	
		p			⁷e	q	u	i	l	a	t	e	r	⁸a	l
		h								c		d	
							⁹f		u		d	
	¹⁰d			¹¹a	l	t	e	r	n	a	t	e
	e		¹²m				a			i	
	c	¹³s	u	b	t	r	a	c	t		v	
	i		l				t				e	
¹⁴s	y	m	m	e	t	r	y				
	a		i				i			
	l		p				o			
			l				n			
			y				s			

Alpha to Omega Activity Pack One Plus

Teacher's Notes — xvii

103 **Science words mix and match: General.** Same as **Exam words mix and match**.

104 **General science words crossword puzzle.** Same as **Exam words crossword puzzle**.

Answer:

			¹e									
			x		²t				³t			
			p		r				r			⁴d
			e	⁵a	p	p	a	r	a	t	u	s	e
			r		n				n			g
			i		s			⁶a	b	s	o	r	b	r
			m		l				p			e
			e		u			⁷m	a	c	h	i	n	e
			n		c		⁸v		r			
		⁹t	h	e	r	m	o	m	e	t	e	r
					n		l		n			
					t		u		t			
							m					
						¹⁰e	q	u	i	p	m	e	n	t

105 **Science words mix and match: Biology.** Same as **Exam words mix and match**.

106 **Biology words crossword puzzle.** Same as **Exam words crossword puzzle**.

Answer:

												¹b
		²e	x	p	a	³n	d			⁴s		i
	⁵t					u			⁶r		u		o
	⁷e	c	o	s	y	s	t	e	m		e		n		l
	m					r			⁸s	k	e	l	e	t	o	n
	p					i			p		i		g
⁹g	e	r	m	i	n	a	t	e		i		g		y
	r					i			r		h		
	a		¹⁰e		o		¹¹h	a	b	i	t	a	t
	t		c		n			t				
	u		o					i				
	r		l				¹²o	x	y	¹³g	e	n
¹⁴r	e	p	r	o	d	u	c	t	i	o	n		r
			g								o
			y								w
											t
											h

Alpha to Omega Activity Pack One Plus

Teacher's Notes

107 **Science words mix and match: Chemistry.** Same as **Exam words mix and match**.

108 **Chemistry words crossword puzzle.** Same as **Exam words crossword puzzle**.

Answer:

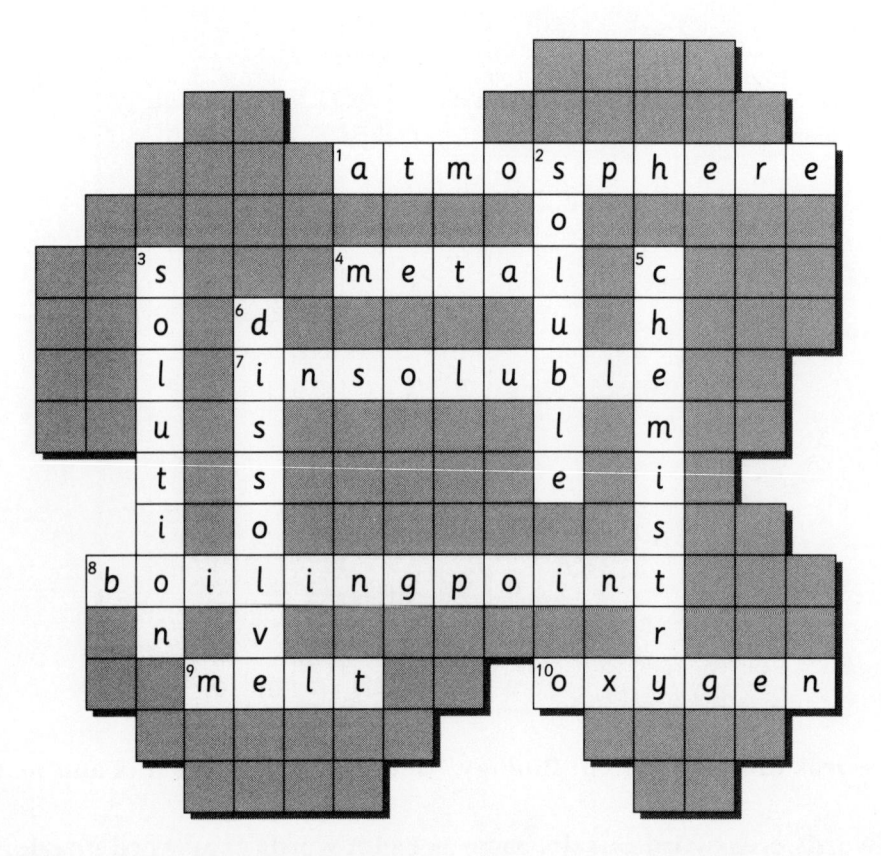

					¹a	t	m	o	²s	p	h	e	r	e
									o					
		³s		⁴m	e	t	a	l		⁵c				
		o	⁶d					u		h				
		l	⁷i	n	s	o	l	u	b	l	e			
		u	s					l		m				
		t	s					e		i				
		i	o							s				
⁸b	o	i	l	i	n	g	p	o	i	n	t			
	n	v								r				
		⁹m	e	l	t			¹⁰o	x	y	g	e	n

109 **Science words mix and match: Physics.** Same as **Exam words mix and match**.

110 **Physics words crossword puzzle:** Same as **Exam words crossword puzzle**.

Answer:

	¹r	²e	f	l	e	c	t
		l					
	³r	e	f	r	a	c	t
		c					
		t					
⁴e	n	e	r	g	y		
		i					
		c					
	⁵w	e	i	g	h	t	
		t					
		y					

Alpha to Omega Activity Pack One Plus

Open syllable words flashcards

a	be	he
me	she	the
we	no	so
go	to	do
I	by	my

2 — Open syllable practice

> Use these words to complete the two exercises below.

a be he me she the we no so go to do I by my

Tracking

> Circle each open syllable word below.

Tom went to the park with his dog. I went to the park too. He met me there and we went to see if we could find the girl in the blue dress. We could not find her so we went to the pond by the hut. Tom asked me to go to the hut to see if she was there. I stood on my toes to look. It was hard to do. No one was there. So I ran back to Tom and we went home.

Fill 'em ups

> Use the words at the top of the page to fill in the blanks below.

"Don't go!" I heard him cry. "What will I ____ without you?"

____ ran ____ him saying, "No, no. I won't ____ yet, but ____ must not be late."

I was sitting in the hut with my cat so they had ____ way of knowing about ____.

"Sit down here ____ my side," he said. "____ must have ____ little chat."

____ cat ran away – and ____ did I.

Alpha to Omega Activity Pack One Plus © Heinemann Educational 1997

Vowels snap 1

a	e	i	o	u
a	e	i	o	u
a	e	i	o	u
a	e	i	o	u
a	e	i	o	u
a	e	i	o	u
a	e	i	o	u
a	e	i	o	u
a	e	i	o	u
a	e	i	o	u
a	e	i	o	u
a	e	i	o	u

© Heinemann Educational 1997

Alpha to Omega Activity Pack One Plus

4 Vowels snap 2

short	sound	name	long
short	sound	name	long
short	sound	name	long
short	sound	name	long
short	sound	name	long
short	sound	name	long
short	sound	name	long
short	sound	name	long
short	sound	name	long
short	sound	name	long
short	sound	name	long
short	sound	name	long

Alpha to Omega Activity Pack One Plus © Heinemann Educational 1997

Short vowels

Short vowel tracking

▶ Track for all the words saying 'e'. Say the word and colour in the 'e'.
Track for all the words saying 'i'. Say the word and colour in the 'i'.
Track for all the words saying 'a'. Say the word and colour in the 'a'.
Track for all the words saying 'u'. Say the word and colour in the 'u'.
Track for all the words saying 'o'. Say the word and colour in the 'o'.

tap   met   fit   top   cut   ten   hop   set

cat   but   sit   fun   bill   tend   grand

hunt   off   next   quit   lash   shut   frost   dripping

bending   batted   munched   stopped   dropping

Short vowel fill 'em ups

▶ Fill in the missing vowels.

They j_mped fr_m the b_ck of the sh_p

into the dark water.

"H_lp! H_lp! We are s_nking."

The shark sl_d by _s they sw_m. It w_nt

b_ck and forth looking _t their b_d luck.

"Wh_ch shall I have first for d_nner?"

▶ What happened next? Write the ending in your exercise book.

© Heinemann Educational 1997   Alpha to Omega Activity Pack One Plus

6 Short vowel tracking

▶ Read the story and track for the short vowel sounds. Highlight or circle each short vowel sound as you find it.

Jack the rat

There was a rat called Jack. He got fed up with living in wet, smelly, pitch black tunnels. He set off and, being smart, landed up in a warm and friendly kitchen. Jack was happy. He hopped and bopped about. He didn't see Tom, the family cat. Tom's eyes had flicked open and he saw grilled rat for dinner. In a flash, he flung himself into space. Jack yelled as ten needle-sharp claws sunk into his smooth, grey, furry coat.

Oscar, the guard dog, woke up. In a fit of temper he dashed into the kitchen and jumped on top of the cat and the rat. Tom forgot his dinner plans. He hissed and spat as Jack fled up the curtain and out of the window.

▶ How will Jack cope? Wait and find out.

Alpha to Omega Activity Pack One Plus © Heinemann Educational 1997

Short vowel fill 'em ups

7

▶ Fill in the missing short vowel sounds to complete the words.
Then read the story.

Jack the rat returns

J__ck the R__t f__ll from the w__ndow. He l__nded __n a p__ddle. He was all m__ddy and feeling s__d and b__d. He s__t up and saw the prettiest l__ttle r__t he had ever seen. "I'm J__nny," she said.

"I'm J__ck. J__st wait a s__cond," he answered. Then he limped to __n overflowing g__tter and he pl__nged into the water. J__nny was so h__ppy when she saw th__s h__ndsome rat p__p out and shake h__mself. "F__llow me," she ordered. "I live in a cosy n__st behind the k__tchen."

They tr__tted off, cr__pt through a tiny hole and __long a n__rrow beam. They met D__d the rat dr__gging a b__g ch__nk of cheese. "T__m __nd Oscar's fight let me gr__b this cheese," he said. "Your b__d luck was our good l__ck. W__ll you stay for s__pper?"

© Heinemann Educational 1997   Alpha to Omega Activity Pack One Plus

8 Short vowels families game

-a-	-a-	-a-	-a-	-a-
cat	cat	cat	cat	cat
hat	**hat**	hat	hat	hat
map	map	**map**	map	map
crab	crab	crab	**crab**	crab
can	can	can	can	**can**

-e-	-e-	-e-	-e-	-e-
bed	bed	bed	bed	bed
fret	**fret**	fret	fret	fret
met	met	**met**	met	met
ten	ten	ten	**ten**	ten
step	step	step	step	**step**

-i-	-i-	-i-	-i-	-i-
fish	fish	fish	fish	fish
bit	**bit**	bit	bit	bit
lick	lick	**lick**	lick	lick
rid	rid	rid	**rid**	rid
pip	pip	pip	pip	**pip**

-o-	-o-	-o-	-o-	-o-
top	top	top	top	top
mop	**mop**	mop	mop	mop
not	not	**not**	not	not
on	on	on	**on**	on
shop	shop	shop	shop	**shop**

-u-	-u-	-u-	-u-	-u-
plum	plum	plum	plum	plum
tub	**tub**	tub	tub	tub
cub	cub	**cub**	cub	cub
us	us	us	**us**	us
cut	cut	cut	cut	**cut**

Alpha to Omega Activity Pack One Plus © Heinemann Educational 1997

'f'/'v'/'th' list 1

▶ Read the words in the lists below. Mark the sound that you **feel** and **hear** in the marking grid on sheet 10.

Initial The sound at the beginning of the word	Final The sound at the end of the word	Medial The sound in the middle of the word
1 the	1 of	1 without
2 for	2 with	2 after
3 very	3 above	3 ever
4 that	4 life	4 mother
5 they	5 live	5 father
6 from	6 have	6 however
7 first	7 earth	7 before
8 five	8 if	8 although
9 there	9 five	9 others
10 through	10 himself	10 several
11 things	11 move	11 other
12 few	12 half	12 given
13 father	13 off	13 different
14 thing	14 give	14 something
15 though	15 both	15 together
16 thirsty	16 fifth	16 nothing

© Heinemann Educational 1997

Alpha to Omega Activity Pack One Plus

10 Student marking grid

▶ Mark the sound that you **hear** and *feel*.

	Initial The sound at the beginning of the word				**Final** The sound at the end of the word				**Medial** The sound in the middle of the word		
	/f/	/v/	/th/		/f/	/v/	/th/		/f/	/v/	/th/
1	☐	☐	☐	1	☐	☐	☐	1	☐	☐	☐
2	☐	☐	☐	2	☐	☐	☐	2	☐	☐	☐
3	☐	☐	☐	3	☐	☐	☐	3	☐	☐	☐
4	☐	☐	☐	4	☐	☐	☐	4	☐	☐	☐
5	☐	☐	☐	5	☐	☐	☐	5	☐	☐	☐
6	☐	☐	☐	6	☐	☐	☐	6	☐	☐	☐
7	☐	☐	☐	7	☐	☐	☐	7	☐	☐	☐
8	☐	☐	☐	8	☐	☐	☐	8	☐	☐	☐
9	☐	☐	☐	9	☐	☐	☐	9	☐	☐	☐
10	☐	☐	☐	10	☐	☐	☐	10	☐	☐	☐
11	☐	☐	☐	11	☐	☐	☐	11	☐	☐	☐
12	☐	☐	☐	12	☐	☐	☐	12	☐	☐	☐
13	☐	☐	☐	13	☐	☐	☐	13	☐	☐	☐
14	☐	☐	☐	14	☐	☐	☐	14	☐	☐	☐
15	☐	☐	☐	15	☐	☐	☐	15	☐	☐	☐
16	☐	☐	☐	16	☐	☐	☐	16	☐	☐	☐

Alpha to Omega Activity Pack One Plus © Heinemann Educational 1997

'f'/'v'/'th' list 2

Mixed

▶ Read the words in the lists below. Mark the sound that you **feel** and **hear** in the marking grid on sheet 12.

1 there
2 earth
3 other
4 father
5 of
6 although
7 fifth
8 leave
9 front
10 mouth
11 fly
12 thousand
13 developed
14 have
15 brother

16 without
17 things
18 both
19 whether
20 three
21 leaf
22 something
23 thought
24 north
25 government
26 thinking
27 various
28 flat
29 thick
30 half

© Heinemann Educational 1997

Alpha to Omega Activity Pack One Plus

12 Student marking grid

▶ Mark the sound that you **hear** and **feel**.

	/f/	/v/	/th/		/f/	/v/	/th/
1	☐	☐	☐	16	☐	☐	☐
2	☐	☐	☐	17	☐	☐	☐
3	☐	☐	☐	18	☐	☐	☐
4	☐	☐	☐	19	☐	☐	☐
5	☐	☐	☐	20	☐	☐	☐
6	☐	☐	☐	21	☐	☐	☐
7	☐	☐	☐	22	☐	☐	☐
8	☐	☐	☐	23	☐	☐	☐
9	☐	☐	☐	24	☐	☐	☐
10	☐	☐	☐	25	☐	☐	☐
11	☐	☐	☐	26	☐	☐	☐
12	☐	☐	☐	27	☐	☐	☐
13	☐	☐	☐	28	☐	☐	☐
14	☐	☐	☐	29	☐	☐	☐
15	☐	☐	☐	30	☐	☐	☐

Alpha to Omega Activity Pack One Plus © Heinemann Educational 1997

'f'/'v'/'th' picture fill 'em ups   13

Write in 'f', 'v' or 'th' to complete the words.

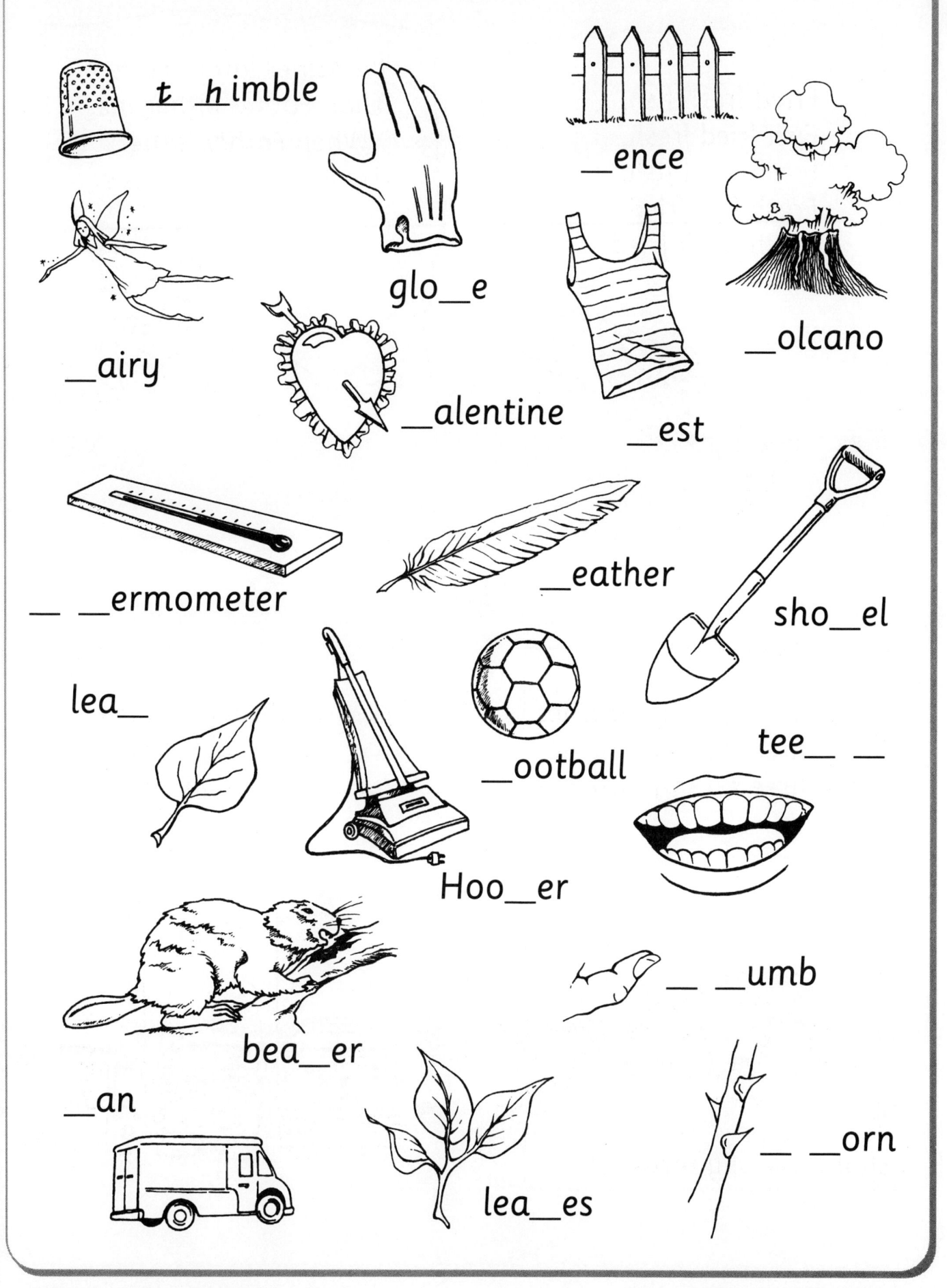

_t_ _h_ imble

__ence

glo__e

__olcano

__airy

__alentine

__est

__ __ermometer

__eather

sho__el

lea__

__ootball

tee__ __

Hoo__er

bea__er

__ __umb

__an

lea__es

__ __orn

© Heinemann Educational 1997   Alpha to Omega Activity Pack One Plus

Tongue twisters

'f'

Fried fresh fish,
Fish fried fresh,
Fresh fried fish,
Fresh fish fried,
Or fish fresh fried.

I'd rather lather Father
Than Father lather me.
When Father lathers
He lathers rather free.

'th'

Thirty-three sly shy thrushes.
Thirty-three sly shy thrushes.
Thirty-three sly shy thrushes.

Three free through trains.
Three free through trains.
Three free through trains.

I shot three shy thrushes.

Alpha to Omega Activity Pack One Plus © Heinemann Educational 1997

Initial blends

15

Underline the beginning letters that are the same in each group of words.

st–	**sm–**	**sl–**	**sc–**	**dr–**
star	smile	sleep	scarf	drum
still	smell	slot	score	drop
stork	smock	slid	Scot	dress
stall	small	slat	scales	draw
staff	smart	slush	scare	drove

sp–	**sn–**	**sw–**	**bl–**	**br–**
spider	snail	swan	blocks	bridge
spill	sniff	swell	black	brass
spell	snug	swim	blot	brave
spin	snore	swat	blush	broke
spot	snag	swore	bluff	brook

Use the beginning letters above to complete the words below.
Write the completed words in a sentence in your exercise book.

s p ider   _ _ ail

_ _ an   _ _ idge

_ _ ocks   _ _ um

_ _ ile   _ _ ar

_ _ arf   _ _ eep

© Heinemann Educational 1997   Alpha to Omega Activity Pack One Plus

16 More smashing initial blends

Fill 'em ups

▶ Read the words below. Trace over the beginning letters with a colour.

cross	skirt	frog	grapes
twins	dwarf	clock	flag
pram	tree	plum	glass

▶ Use the beginning letters above to complete the words below. Write the completed words in your exercise book. Read them as you write.

c l ock 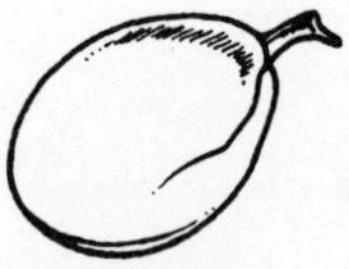   __ __ um

__ __ oss   __ __ ass

__ __ ee    __ __ ag

__ __ apes    __ __ am

__ __ og    __ __ irt

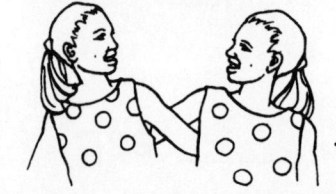

__ __ ins    __ __ arf

Alpha to Omega Activity Pack One Plus © Heinemann Educational 1997

Tracking for triple blends

17

▶ Go over the triple blends in a colour. Say the sound as you colour.

thr   fl   shr   fr   thr   pl   st   spr   fr   sm   spl

sp   str   dr   squ   br   spl   gr   thr   gl   scr

▶ Colour all the 'spl's and say their sound.

squash   split   three   splint   sprint   shred

splendid   screw   strip   scrap   throw   spring

▶ Say the triple blend words.

shrink   slap   thrash   free   strap   squirt   flag

scrub   splutter   print   strike   swim   spree

▶ Track the 'str's, saying the single sound.

str   st   spl   str   str   scr   thr   str

st   str   st   str   spl   spr   str   squ

▶ Colour the 'str's and say the word.

string   scrap   three   stroke   stripe   stand

strand   score   scrimp   strong   stress   splash

© Heinemann Educational 1997   Alpha to Omega Activity Pack One Plus

18 Assimilation

-ng -nd -nt -nk -nch -mp -mb

▶ Read the words below. Listen for the sound of the 'n' and the 'm'.
Use the words to fill in the blanks in the poem.

**branch sing campground tent morning
ding swing lunch bent**

Let's go down to the _____ and pitch our _____.
We can hang our _____ from the _____ which is _____.
We will wake in the _____ when the birds start to _____
and munch our _____ when Pam's watch goes _____.

▶ Fill in the blanks below with the word which is spelled correctly.

1 There is a _____ (**bupy, bunpy, bumpy**), lumpy _____ (**clunp, clop, clump**) of grass under my _____ (**brand, pran, brant**) new tent.

2 Can you _____ (**sing, sink, sig**) me a _____ (**sog, song, son**) while you jump up and wave your _____ (**hand, hant, hand**)?

3 _____ (**pink, ping, pic**) is a _____ (**tint, tin, tind**) of red.

4 The _____ (**betch, bensh, bench**) is a bit _____ (**danp, damp, dap**) so I will stand while the _____ (**band, bad, bamd**) plays.

5 I _____ (**want, wat, what**) to munch on a _____ (**buntch, bunsh, bunch**) of grapes after _____ (**lunch, luntch, luch**).

6 I _____ (**thinck, think, theek**) I spent 50p when I _____ (**wet, whent, went**) to the shops with _____ (**grampa, gradpa, grandpa**).

Alpha to Omega Activity Pack One Plus   © Heinemann Educational 1997

Finding the final blends

▶ Read the sounds below. When they come at the end of a word, they are called 'final blends'.

-st -ct -lt -lf -lm
-sk -sp -lk -xt -lp

▶ Read the following words from left to write and circle the final blends with a colour.

rut	tut	me(lt)	met	fell	felt	belt	bet
sip	ask	dust	task	tan	quit	whip	wisp
crisp	rip	trip	hut	wilt	sulk	let	thrust
set	stet	best	thrust	hiss	loss	toss	test
net	nut	but	nest	wit	lit	glitter	best
lift	act	fact	face	stop	step	crest	left
next	nix	cram	frost	swim	ram	must
strum	hum	strap	milk	left	trust	self
than	shed	glad	hulk	zest	shelf	flip
bulk	have	must	shut	shell	star	wet	flan
plum	tram	this	flag	gut	gust	silk	crust
have	ten	three	talk	dust	lest	help

20 | Final blends and assimilations

Mix and match

▶ Match the beginning of each of the following words with an ending to make a word. The same ending may be used more than once.

1	be_____		**mb**
2	re_____		**ft**
3	thu_____		**lt**
4	she_____		**nd**
5	stri_____		**mp**
6	li_____		**ng**
7	la_____		**lk**
8	mi_____		**nch**
9	be_____		**nt**
10	si_____		**lf**
11	te_____		**ng**
12	ha_____		
13	sta_____		
14	bri_____		

Alpha to Omega Activity Pack One Plus © Heinemann Educational 1997

The battle of the blends balloons 1 — 21

Equipment:
- A die showing ones and twos only.
- Counters or markers.
- Pencil and paper for each player.
- A stopwatch (optional).

NB **TH** = **T**eacher's **H**andicap

How to play:

1. Each player takes a turn to spin the spinner.
2. The first player moves forward the number of spaces s/he won on the first spin.
3. Each time a player lands on a *forfeit* space, s/he picks a *forfeit* card and writes words using the sound pattern on the card.
4. For every group of words spelled correctly, the player moves forward two spaces (**TH** – For every group of words correctly spelled, go forward one space).
5. To make the game more exciting, use a stopwatch and allow 10 seconds per word. If the player takes longer, s/he should only go forward one space (**TH** – do not move forward at all).
6. The first person to reach the finish wins.

sp Write 4 words TH: Write 6 words	**st** Write 4 words TH: Write 6 words	**sc** Write 1 word TH: Write 3 words	**sm** Write 5 words TH: Write 7 words
sn Write 3 words TH: Write 6 words	**sl** Write 4 words TH: Write 8 words	**sw** Write 3 words TH: Write 5 words	**tw** Write 2 words TH: Write 5 words
dw Write 1 word TH: Write 2 words	**bl** Write 5 words TH: Write 10 words	**cl** Write 4 words TH: Write 8 words	**gl** Write 3 words TH: Write 5 words
fl Write 5 words TH: Write 10 words	**pr** Write 4 words TH: Write 8 words	**br** Write 3 words TH: Write 6 words	**tr** Write 3 words TH: Write 6 words
dr Write 5 words TH: Write 6 words	**pl** Write 4 words TH: Write 8 words	**cr** Write 3 words TH: Write 6 words	**gr** Write 3 words TH: Write 6 words
fr Write 3 words TH: Write 6 words	**thr** Write 2 words TH: Write 4 words	**spr** Write 2 words TH: Write 4 words	**squ** Write 1 word TH: Write 3 words
pl Write 1 word TH: Write 3 words	**shr** Write 1 word TH: Write 3 words	**str** Write 2 words TH: Write 4 words	**scr** Write 2 words TH: Write 4 words

© Heinemann Educational 1997 Alpha to Omega Activity Pack One Plus

22 The battle of the blends balloons 2

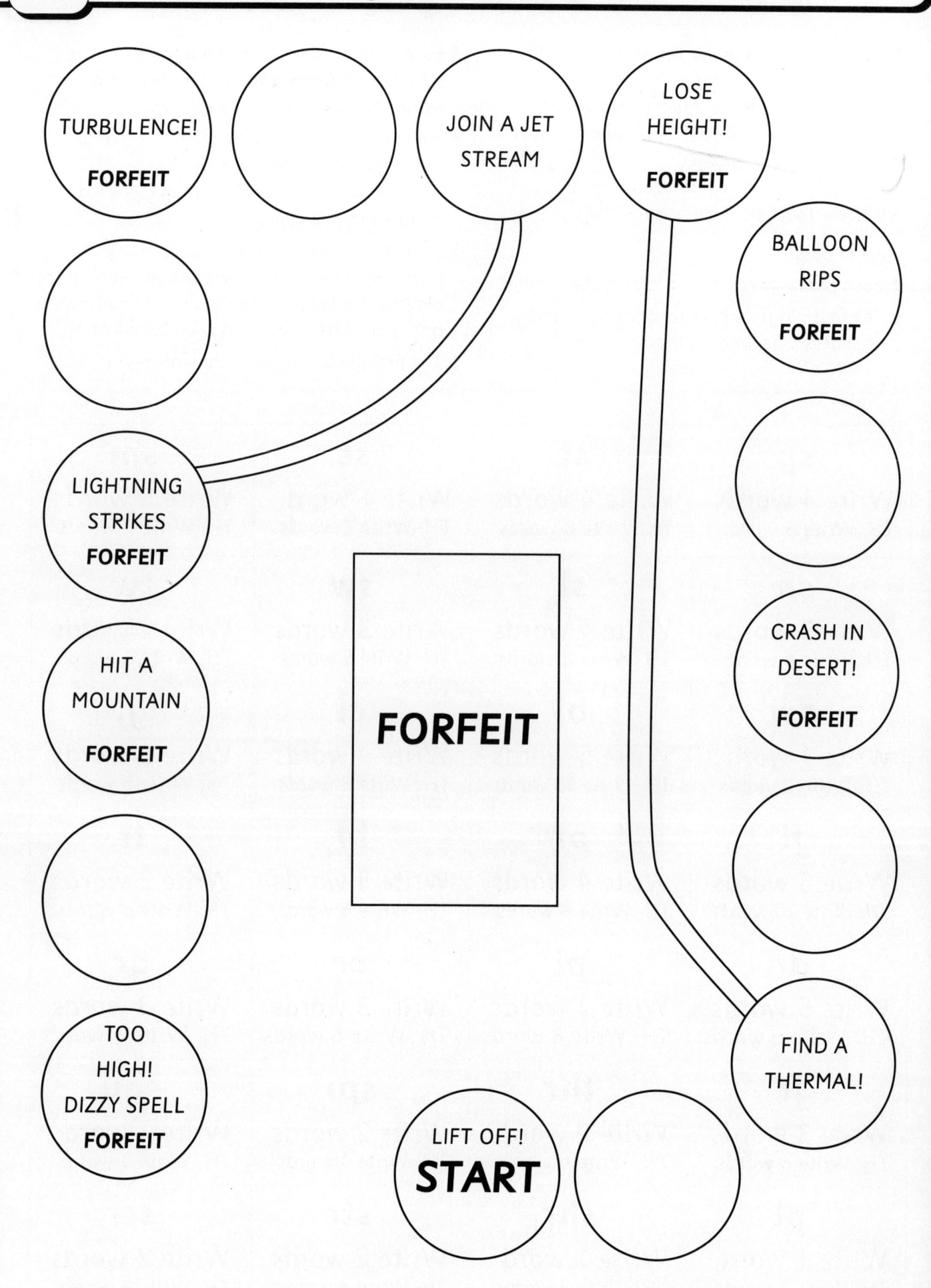

- TURBULENCE! **FORFEIT**
- JOIN A JET STREAM
- LOSE HEIGHT! **FORFEIT**
- BALLOON RIPS **FORFEIT**
- LIGHTNING STRIKES **FORFEIT**
- **FORFEIT**
- CRASH IN DESERT! **FORFEIT**
- HIT A MOUNTAIN **FORFEIT**
- TOO HIGH! DIZZY SPELL **FORFEIT**
- FIND A THERMAL!
- LIFT OFF! **START**

Alpha to Omega Activity Pack One Plus © Heinemann Educational 1997

The battle of the blends balloons 3 | 23

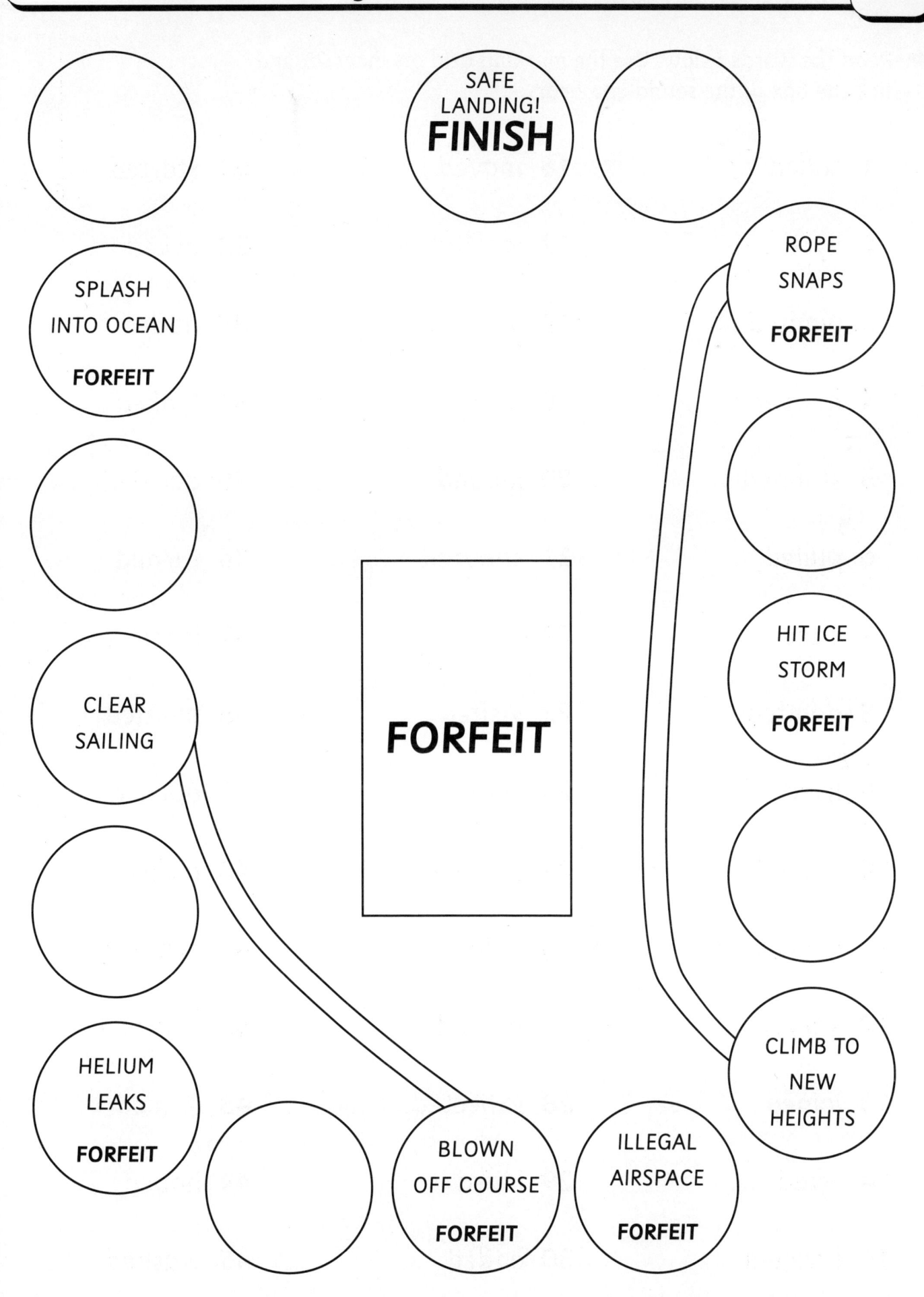

SAFE LANDING! **FINISH**

SPLASH INTO OCEAN **FORFEIT**

ROPE SNAPS **FORFEIT**

CLEAR SAILING

FORFEIT

HIT ICE STORM **FORFEIT**

HELIUM LEAKS **FORFEIT**

BLOWN OFF COURSE **FORFEIT**

ILLEGAL AIRSPACE **FORFEIT**

CLIMB TO NEW HEIGHTS

© Heinemann Educational 1997

Alpha to Omega Activity Pack One Plus

24 'ed' list

▶ Read the words below. Use the marking grid on sheet 25 and tick the box of the sound you hear.

1 called	16 moved	31 started
2 lived	17 walked	32 asked
3 wanted	18 jumped	33 added
4 happened	19 used	34 looked
5 stopped	20 played	35 decided
6 pulled	21 shouted	36 turned
7 cried	22 helped	37 interested
8 pointed	23 visited	38 planted
9 liked	24 changed	39 opened
10 waited	25 finished	40 picked
11 showed	26 painted	41 climbed
12 stayed	27 missed	42 believed
13 joined	28 expected	43 landed
14 lifted	29 loved	44 hoped
15 listened	30 ended	45 washed

Alpha to Omega Activity Pack One Plus © Heinemann Educational 1997

Student marking grid

25

▶ Tick the box of the sound you hear.

	/t/	/d/	/id/		/t/	/d/	/id/		/t/	/d/	/id/
1	☐	☐	☐	16	☐	☐	☐	31	☐	☐	☐
2	☐	☐	☐	17	☐	☐	☐	32	☐	☐	☐
3	☐	☐	☐	18	☐	☐	☐	33	☐	☐	☐
4	☐	☐	☐	19	☐	☐	☐	34	☐	☐	☐
5	☐	☐	☐	20	☐	☐	☐	35	☐	☐	☐
6	☐	☐	☐	21	☐	☐	☐	36	☐	☐	☐
7	☐	☐	☐	22	☐	☐	☐	37	☐	☐	☐
8	☐	☐	☐	23	☐	☐	☐	38	☐	☐	☐
9	☐	☐	☐	24	☐	☐	☐	39	☐	☐	☐
10	☐	☐	☐	25	☐	☐	☐	40	☐	☐	☐
11	☐	☐	☐	26	☐	☐	☐	41	☐	☐	☐
12	☐	☐	☐	27	☐	☐	☐	42	☐	☐	☐
13	☐	☐	☐	28	☐	☐	☐	43	☐	☐	☐
14	☐	☐	☐	29	☐	☐	☐	44	☐	☐	☐
15	☐	☐	☐	30	☐	☐	☐	45	☐	☐	☐

© Heinemann Educational 1997

Alpha to Omega Activity Pack One Plus

26 'ed' endings 1

▶ Write the past tense of the given word on the line provided.

play
played
sounds like /d/

wait
___
sounds like /id/

walk
___
sounds like /t/

jump
___
sounds like /t/

want
___
sounds like /id/

like
___
sounds like /d/

help
___
sounds like /t/

add
___
sounds like /id/

live
___
sounds like /d/

turn
___
sounds like /d/

start
___
sounds like /id/

miss
___
sounds like /t/

ask
___
sounds like /t/

look
___
sounds like /d/

paint
___
sounds like /ed/

Alpha to Omega Activity Pack One Plus   © Heinemann Educational 1997

'ed' endings 2

▶ Write the past tense of the given word on the line provided.

stay ___ sounds like /d/

hope ___ sounds like /t/

visit ___ sounds like /id/

pick ___ sounds like /t/

lift ___ sounds like /id/

pull ___ sounds like /d/

plant ___ sounds like /id/

open ___ sounds like /d/

stop ___ sounds like /t/

wash ___ sounds like /t/

land ___ sounds like /id/

love ___ sounds like /d/

call ___ sounds like /d/

end ___ sounds like /id/

hope ___ sounds like /t/

28 'ed' proofreading

▶ Read the story below and correct the past tense endings. Write the corrected story on the lines provided.

He pickt up his bag and startid to walk across the street. Someone calld to him to stop. They had just paintid the lines. He turnd and lookd. He jumpt over the shiny lines and dropt his bag. It landid in the yellow paint. He pulld it out of the paint and liftid it up. Then he stopt to look at his yellow bag. He hopd his mother would not mind when he askt her if it could be washt.

Alpha to Omega Activity Pack One Plus © Heinemann Educational 1997

Word sums

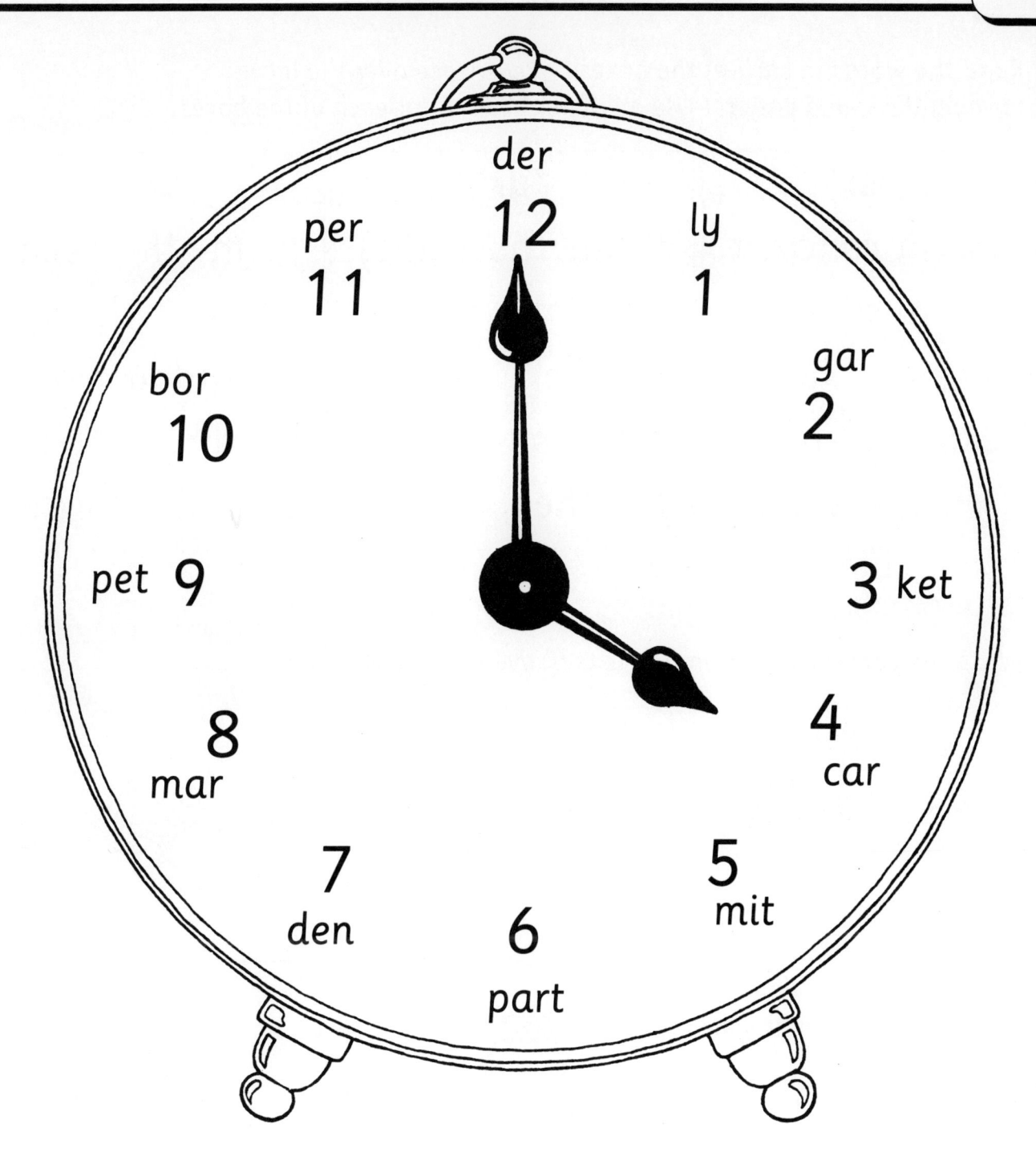

29

Clock face with words at positions:
- 12: der
- 1: ly
- 2: gar
- 3: ket
- 4: car
- 5: mit
- 6: part
- 7: den
- 8: mar
- 9: pet
- 10: bor
- 11: per

1 What word is it at 10.00? _____
2 What word is it at 4.45? _____
3 What word is it at 8.15? _____
4 What word is it at 11.25? _____
5 What word is it at 2.35? _____
6 What word is it at 6.05? _____

© Heinemann Educational 1997   Alpha to Omega Activity Pack One Plus

30 'er' 'ur' 'ir' have the same sound

▶ Read the words in each of the boxes below. Trace over the letters forming the sound pattern. Use a different colour for each of the boxes.

'er'	'ur'	'ir'
term concert	turn Thursday	firm thirteen
fern smaller	return purse	birth thirty
server herb	nurse burst	birthday sir
expert enter	blur murmur	bird first
serve verse	further curl	girl third

▶ Write the correct word from the lists above under each picture.

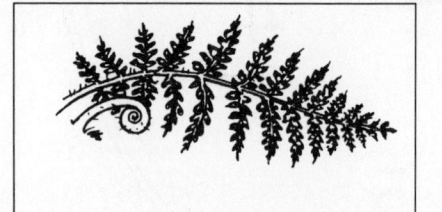

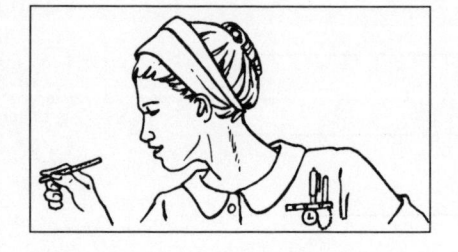

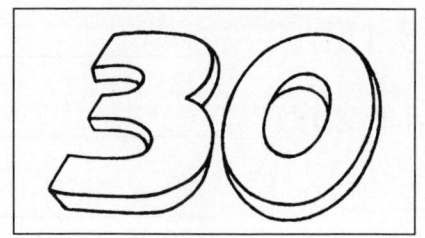

Alpha to Omega Activity Pack One Plus © Heinemann Educational 1997

'er' 'ur' 'ir' fill 'em ups

Underline the word in brackets which has the correct spelling.
Then write the completed sentence on the line below.

1. There were (**therty, thirty, thurty**) (**birds, berds, burds**) chirping in the lemon tree next door.

2. It is your (**turn, tern, tirn**), sir, to (**sirve, surve, serve**) the tea from the (**silvir, silver, silvur**) pot.

3. The (**nerse, nurse, nirse**) is (**expirt, expert, expurt**) at treating (**birns, berns, burns**).

4. Jake was the (**first, furst, ferst**) to (**burst, berst, birst**) a balloon at Pam's (**thirteenth, therteenth, thurteenth**) birthday party.

5. The (**sittur, sittir, sitter**) will come the (**third, thurd, therd**) (**Thersday, Thirsday, Thursday**) of every month.

6. Mum has a wonderful (**herb, hirb, hurb**) garden surrounded by (**ferns, firns, furns**).

32 Top of the Tower

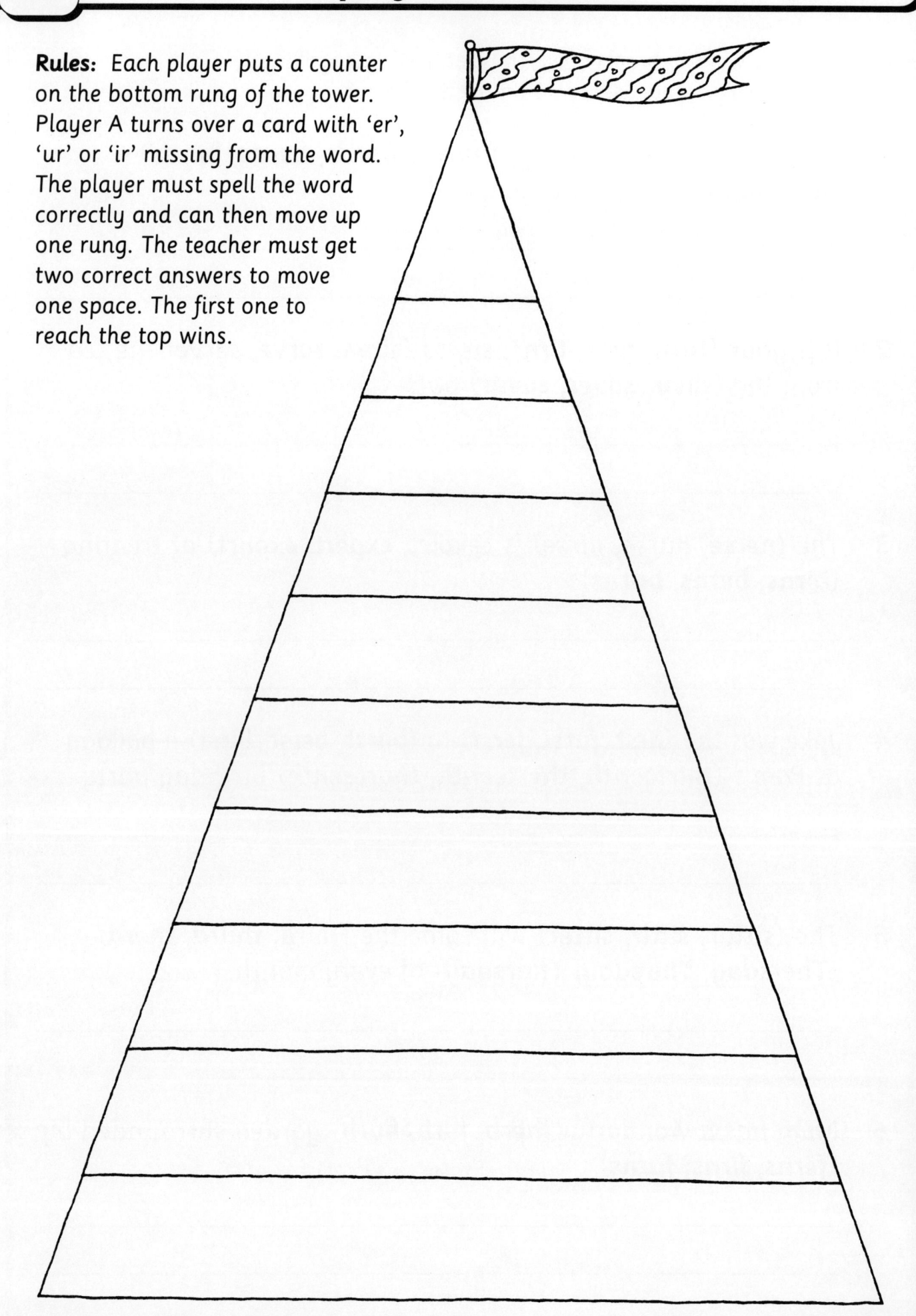

Rules: Each player puts a counter on the bottom rung of the tower. Player A turns over a card with 'er', 'ur' or 'ir' missing from the word. The player must spell the word correctly and can then move up one rung. The teacher must get two correct answers to move one space. The first one to reach the top wins.

Alpha to Omega Activity Pack One Plus © Heinemann Educational 1997

Top of the tower cards   33

t _ _ m	t _ _ n	th _ _ ty
s _ _ ve	ret _ _ n	s _ _
silv _ _	n _ _ se	f _ _ m
exp _ _ t	b _ _ st	b _ _ th
f _ _ n	bl _ _	b _ _ thday
v _ _ se	f _ _ ther	b _ _ d
small _ _	m _ _ mur	f _ _ st
ent _ _	Th _ _ sday	th _ _ d
conc _ _ t	p _ _ se	st _ _
h _ _ b	b _ _ n	ch _ _ p

© Heinemann Educational 1997   Alpha to Omega Activity Pack One Plus

34   Wave the witch's wand

▶ Read the following sentence.

Walter **wa**nts to **wa**nder the **wor**ld and **wor**k in the **war**m sunshine.

▶ Read the words below, then use a coloured pen to trace the
war, **wor** and **wa** patterns.

war– (sounds like /or/)	**wor–** (sounds like /er/)	**wa–** (sounds like /o/)
award	worm	wand
reward	work	swan
warn	word	want
warm	world	wash

▶ Read the paragraph below and fill in each blank with the correct word.

The chickens were digging for _____ (**worms, werms**) while Mrs Jones _____ (**wos, was**) hanging out the _____ (**washing, woshing**). The baby _____ (**swons, swans**) liked their new _____ (**world, werld**). They watched everyone _____ (**werking, working**) very _____ (**had, hard**). There was a _____ (**warning, worning**) on the radio about a large _____ (**storm, sterm**) forming. The _____ (**famer, farmer**) was glad he had a large barn to keep his animals _____ (**worm, warm**).

Alpha to Omega Activity Pack One Plus   © Heinemann Educational 1997

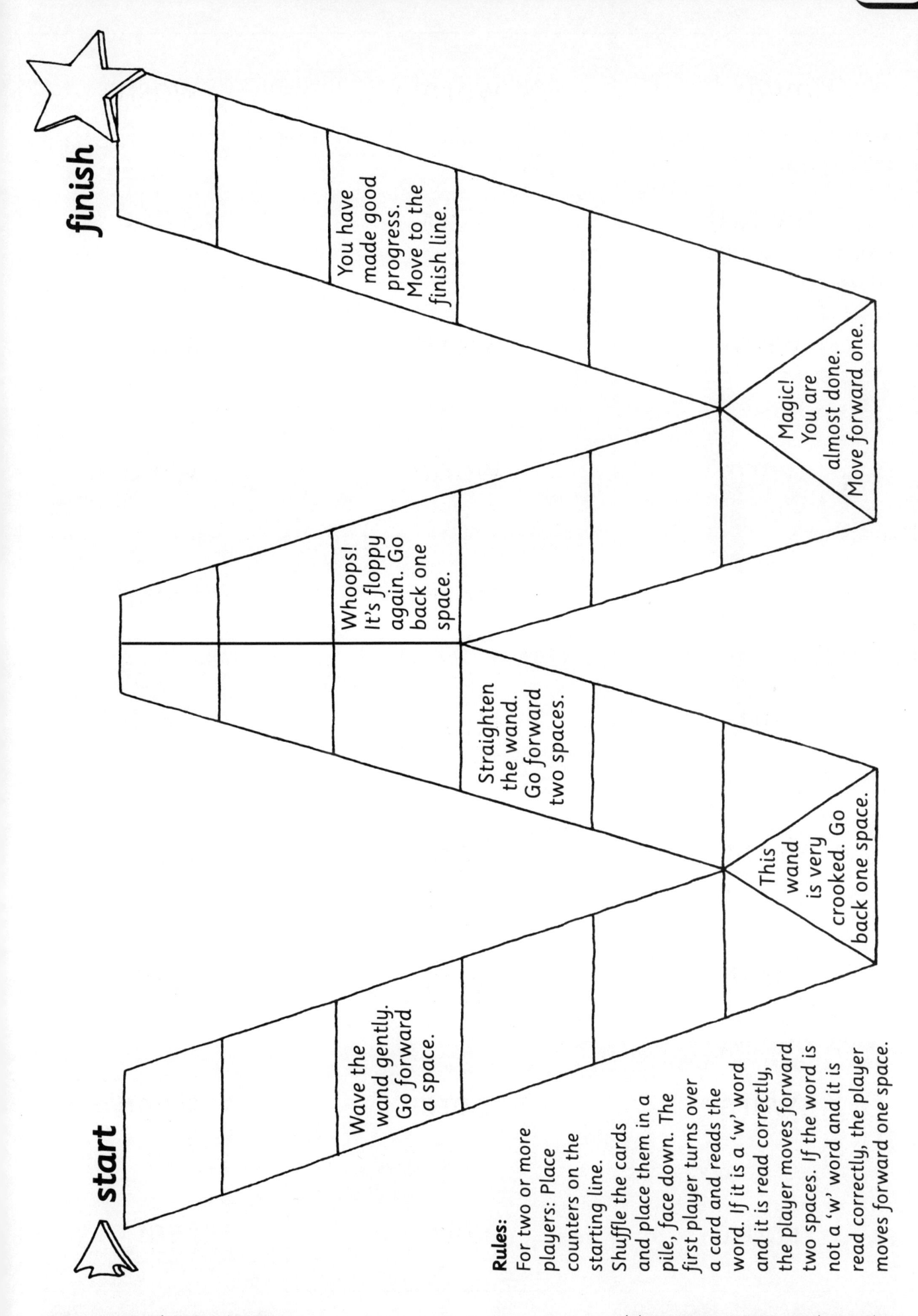

Wave the wand

35

finish

start

You have made good progress. Move to the finish line.

Magic! You are almost done. Move forward one.

Whoops! It's floppy again. Go back one space.

Straighten the wand. Go forward two spaces.

This wand is very crooked. Go back one space.

Wave the wand gently. Go forward a space.

Rules:
For two or more players: Place counters on the starting line. Shuffle the cards and place them in a pile, face down. The first player turns over a card and reads the word. If it is a 'w' word and it is read correctly, the player moves forward two spaces. If the word is not a 'w' word and it is read correctly, the player moves forward one space.

© Heinemann Educational 1997

Alpha to Omega Activity Pack One Plus

36 Wave the wand flashcards

award	worm	wash
reward	work	wand
warn	word	swan
warm	world	want
harp	cork	wand
lark	storm	flash
farm	born	dash
dart	fork	bat
swarm	pore	stand
chart	corn	sat

The flossy families game 1

37

ss ss	ss ss	ss ss
The 'ss' Family gla**ss** **glass** loss miss fuss less	**The 'ss' Family** lo**ss** glass **loss** miss fuss less	**The 'ss' Family** mi**ss** glass loss **miss** fuss less
ss ss	ss ss	ss ss
ss ss	ss ss	ss ss
The 'ss' Family fu**ss** glass loss miss **fuss** less	**The 'ss' Family** le**ss** glass loss miss fuss **less**	**The 'ss' Family** **Rule Card** glass — One syllable word one short vowel ends with /s/ – write 'ss.' loss miss fuss less Exceptions: is, has, his, yes, thus, this, us, goes, bus.
ss ss	ss ss	ss ss
ll ll	ll ll	ll ll
The 'll' Family fi**ll** **tall** well fill doll dull	**The 'll' Family** we**ll** tall **well** fill doll dull	**The 'll' Family** ta**ll** tall well **fill** doll dull
ll ll	ll ll	ll ll

© Heinemann Educational 1997

Alpha to Omega Activity Pack One Plus

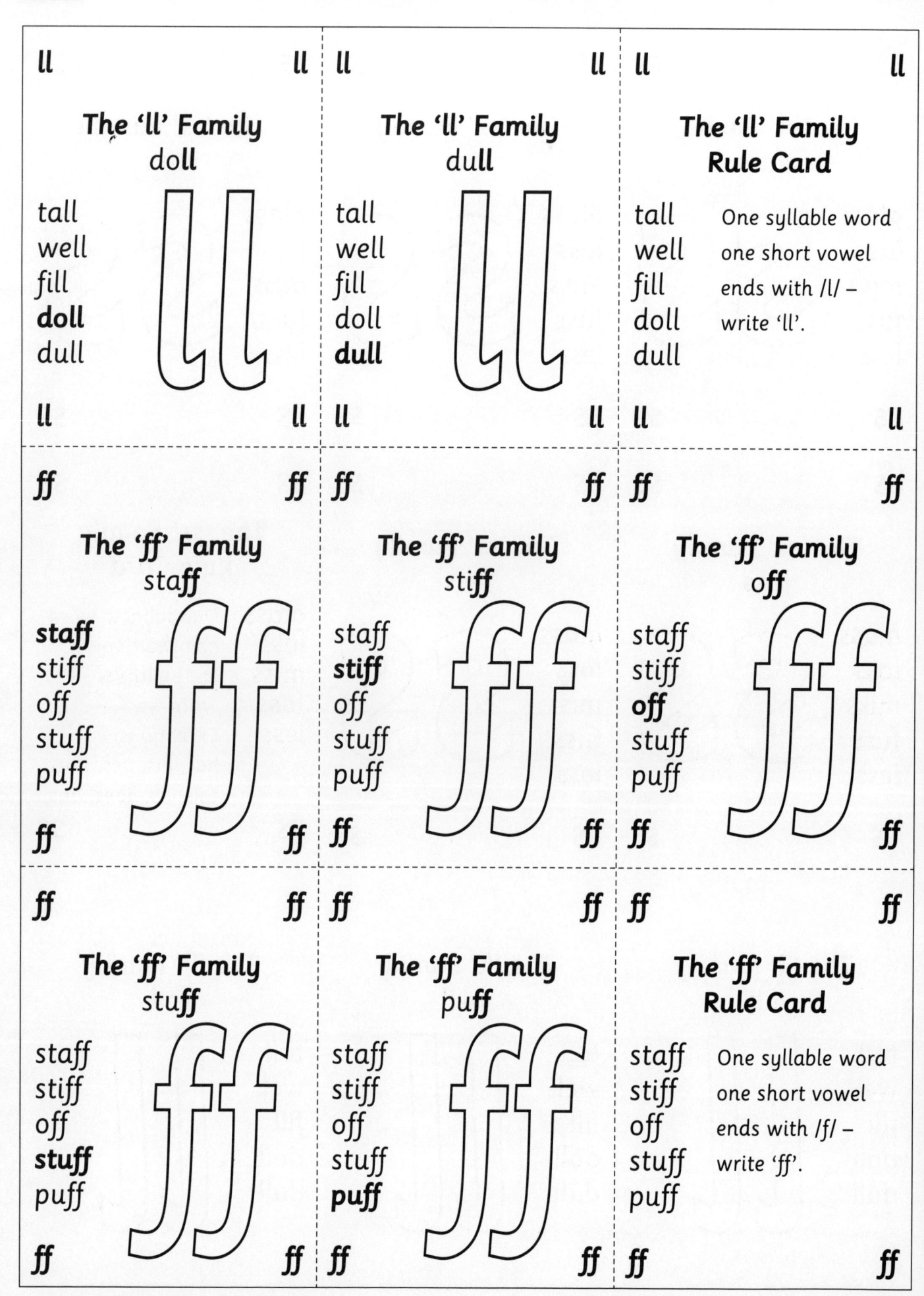

38 The flossy families game 2

Card 1 (ll)

The 'll' Family
doll

tall
well
fill
doll
dull

Card 2 (ll)

The 'll' Family
dull

tall
well
fill
doll
dull

Card 3 (ll) — Rule Card

The 'll' Family
Rule Card

tall
well
fill
doll
dull

One syllable word
one short vowel
ends with /l/ –
write 'll'.

Card 4 (ff)

The 'ff' Family
staff

staff
stiff
off
stuff
puff

Card 5 (ff)

The 'ff' Family
stiff

staff
stiff
off
stuff
puff

Card 6 (ff)

The 'ff' Family
off

staff
stiff
off
stuff
puff

Card 7 (ff)

The 'ff' Family
stuff

staff
stiff
off
stuff
puff

Card 8 (ff)

The 'ff' Family
puff

staff
stiff
off
stuff
puff

Card 9 (ff) — Rule Card

The 'ff' Family
Rule Card

staff
stiff
off
stuff
puff

One syllable word
one short vowel
ends with /f/ –
write 'ff'.

Alpha to Omega Activity Pack One Plus © Heinemann Educational 1997

The flossy families game 3

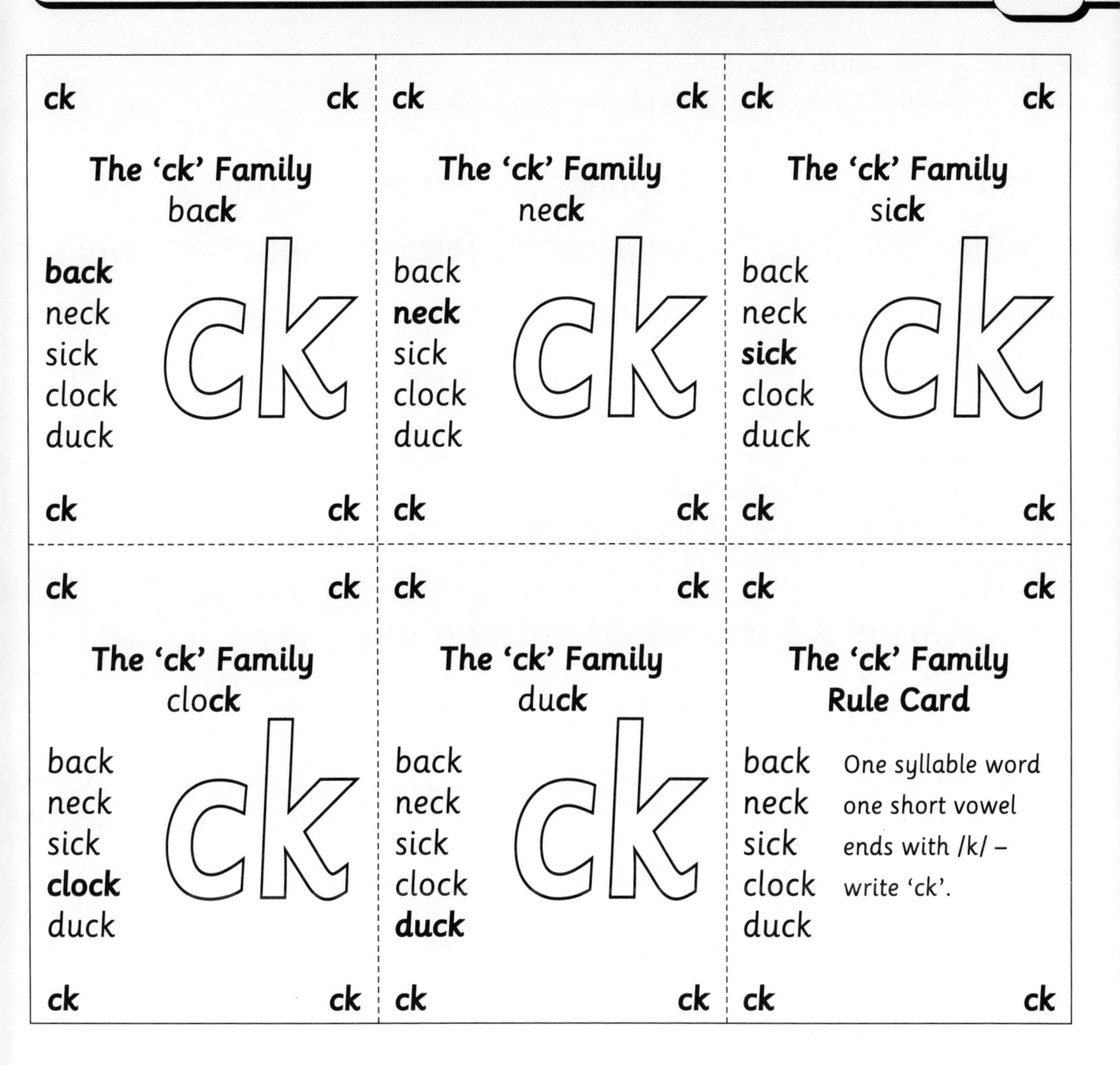

39

---

ck ck	ck ck	ck ck
The 'ck' Family ba**ck** **back** neck sick clock duck	**The 'ck' Family** ne**ck** back **neck** sick clock duck	**The 'ck' Family** si**ck** back neck **sick** clock duck
ck ck	ck ck	ck ck
ck ck	ck ck	ck ck
The 'ck' Family clo**ck** back neck sick **clock** duck	**The 'ck' Family** du**ck** back neck sick clock **duck**	**The 'ck' Family** Rule Card back — One syllable word neck — one short vowel sick — ends with /k/ – clock — write 'ck'. duck
ck ck	ck ck	ck ck

© Heinemann Educational 1997   Alpha to Omega Activity Pack One Plus

40 'll' tracking and cloze poem

▶ Track for the words ending in 'll'.
Fill in the 'll' as you read the words.

belt	all	stopped	halt	tilt	fall
fault	hill	small	felt	spilt	wall
hilt	spell	welt	help	belt	wilt
well	stilts	ill	kilt	swell	thrill	wilt

▶ Fill in the missing words in the poem below.
All of the missing words are in the tracking above.

This is a poem about nothing at _____.

Just be careful that you don't _____.

You might get a *thrill*

Cycling fast down_____

Or you might feel very *small*

When you ride into a _____.

Your teacher might say that you know how

to _____

All of those words that end in 'll',

So to all of you who have done so _____,

Congratulations. I think you're *swell*.

Alpha to Omega Activity Pack One Plus © Heinemann Educational 1997

'ss' tracking and cloze poem — 41

▶ Read the words below and track for all the words with 'ss', filling in the 'ss' with a coloured pen. Use a different coloured pen to track for the words with one 's'.

boss	is	visits	cross	first	fuss
wish	us	bus	lass	class	pass
has	stress	must	this	list	best	mess
his	last	kiss	lots	bliss	crust

▶ Now complete the poem below by filling in the blanks. All of the words you need are 'ss' or 's' words from the tracking above.

Bess is the *boss*

And she gets _____.

She makes a great _____

When we get on the _____.

At school, she comes into the _____

And says she will _____.

I really must _____

That this lass is a _____.

Throw her a _____

and all will be *bliss*.

42 'ff' tracking and cloze poem

▶ Read the words as you track for the 'ff' words. Colour the 'ff'.

giraffe	half	cliff	cough	stiff	wolf
sniff	calf	whiff	of	laugh	coffee
toffee	off	puff	after	stuff

▶ Read the poem. Complete it by filling in the blank spaces.
Use words from the tracking above.

The _____
had a laugh
As he clung to the _____,
With his neck very _____,
And he took a deep _____.
"What, on earth,
is that smelly _____?
It isn't _____,
It can't be _____.
What, oh what, can this be?
I'd better be _____
Before I cough
Not another _____
Of that awful _____".

Alpha to Omega Activity Pack One Plus © Heinemann Educational 1997

'ck' tracking and cloze poem   43

▶ Read the words as you track for 'ck'. Colour in the 'ck's as you find them.

take	stock	poke	clock	sock	rice
luck	tick	make	rocket		bike
stuck	stick	block	lake		attack
pick	rich	thick	lock	ticket	back

▶ Now complete the poem below by filling in the 'ck' words. They are all in the tracking above.

It's time to take *stock*

of the time on the _____.

We won't have much _____

If we really get _____.

We can pack and be quick

Take clothes that are _____.

You're on a good *wicket*

If you stick with this _____.

© Heinemann Educational 1997   Alpha to Omega Activity Pack One Plus

44 Flossy words multiple choice

▶ Read each sentence. Choose the correct spelling of the word and write it in the space provided.

1. The _____ (**clase, clas, class**) waited restlessly while the _____ (**staff, stafe, staf**) had a meeting.

2. "Bring _____ (**bacc, bake, back**) my book!" he cried as he walked away in a _____ (**huf, huff, hufe**).

3. The _____ (**truck, truke, truc**) in the yard is reversing into the _____ (**hil, hile, hill**) and will get _____ (**stuk, stuck, stook**) in the _____ (**muck, muke, mkk**).

4. Put that _____ (**stufe, stuf, stuff**) in the _____ (**pocit, pocket, poket**) with my _____ (**ticket, tikit, ticet**) and I shall _____ (**stik, stike, stick**) it in the file when I get home.

5. When the children made hot _____ (**crose, cros, cross**) buns, candy _____ (**floss, flos, flose**) and _____ (**tofe, toofee, toffee**), the kitchen was a _____ (**tiky, sticky, stickey**) mess.

Alpha to Omega Activity Pack One Plus   © Heinemann Educational 1997

An odd flossy ode

▶ Read the words and highlight the flossy endings.

impress   bluff   tell   luck   puff

stuck   skill   will   mess   well

▶ Use the words above to complete the poem below.

To get this far, you have done very _____

To complete the silly poems I _____.

You may have had a bit of _____

But some of you, I'm sure, got _____.

The flossy words take a bit of _____

Which I know you have and always _____.

Keep up the practice and don't make a _____

Think of the teachers that you will _____.

Finished is the huff and _____

And I must go and call your _____.

© Heinemann Educational 1997   Alpha to Omega Activity Pack One Plus

Soft 'c'

–ce– –ci– –cy–

▶ Read the words below. Trace over the soft 'c' spelling pattern for each word. Use a different colour for each of the three patterns.

centipede	circle	cycle
centre	city	cyclone
century	cinema	cylinder
certain	pencil	cymbals
centimetre	decide	cypress

Tracking for **soft 'c'** and /k/

▶ Circle in red the words below that contain a soft 'c'.
▶ Circle in blue the words below that contain a /k/ sound.

cotton   alcove   trace   cake   parcel   dice   scorn   clear   recent

cinder   cannot   fact   placing   certain   cypress   record   grocer

concur   circle   cycle   doctor   candid   cease   crease   camp   cramp

pencil   coconut   chocolate   cricket   local   focus   contest   century

city   collect   cygnet   lance   prance   dancing   cylinder   chicken

Alpha to Omega Activity Pack One Plus © Heinemann Educational 1997

'c' or 'k'

That was a nice kick

▶ Fill in the missing letters with either a 'c' or a 'k'.
Write the completed sentence on the line below.

1 Carol is a __een cricketer.
_____

2 The __ettle in the __itchen was __old.
_____

3 __an you lift a one __ilo sack of __otton?
_____

4 The sale of the __entury is __ertain to be a suc__ess.
_____

5 The i__e cream __one had __oconut fla__es and chun__s of sweet, dar__ cho__olate.
_____
_____

6 The __aptain of the lo__al team made the best __ick of the game.
_____
_____

7 The __at had five __ittens with black spots.
_____

8 The __yclist took a short __ut to the __ity __entre.
_____

© Heinemann Educational 1997   Alpha to Omega Activity Pack One Plus

48 Camping or not

'c', 'k' or 'ck'

▶ Read the following sentences. Underline the words in brackets which have the correct spelling.

1. It was the day of the (**camping, kamping, ckamping**) trip and the (**clouds, klouds, cklouds**) above were very (**darck, dare, dark**).

2. The air was (**cool, kool, ckool**) and there was a breeze stirring the tall (**klumps, clumps, cklumps**) of grass.

3. Carl and Cindy (**clutched, klutched, cklutched**) their blankets and their (**ruksaks, rucksacks, rucsacs**) and (**walcked, waked, walked**) to the (**karavan, caravan, ckarevan**) which was (**parked, parcked, parkked**) at the front gate.

'c', 'k' or 'ck' proofreading

▶ Read the next part of the story. Find the spelling errors in the passage. Write the corrected version in your exercise book.

They cheked the cloc in the citchen. They had to decide quikly what to do. It was riscy setting out in this weather and they didn't licke the idea of a wet weeck. This was the worst luk. This day had been marcked on their kalendars for ages. A week in a kabin in the centre of a storm with the rain koming down in bukets was no fun, but a week in a tent was the worst thing they could thinck of.

Alpha to Omega Activity Pack One Plus © Heinemann Educational 1997

Mar__'s __rossword

'c' 'ck' 'k'

circus ice centre kick kite call sit century kid circle kiss bicycle cook kicks city sick

Across

3 Touch with your lips
5 Frozen water
6 100 years
7 Baby goat
10 What you do at the stove
12 Middle
13 A telephone _ al _
14 Mark _ _ _ _ _ the football.
15 You fly it in the wind at the end of a string.

Down

1 I want to ride my _ _ _ _ _ _ _.
2 London is a big _ _ _ _.
4 I _ _ _ in my chair.
6 A round shape which we draw
8 There will be a trapeze artist at the _ _ _ _ _ _.
9 He felt ill and was _ _ _ _ all over the floor.
11 Jack wants to _ _ _ _ the football.
12 Same as '6 down'

50 Gentle soft 'g'

– ge – – gi – – gy –

▶ Read the words in each box out loud. Trace over the letters forming the sound pattern. Use a different colour for each of the three spelling patterns.

gem    **gi**ant    **gy**mnast

general danger	ginger logic	gym
gentle enlarge	gigantic gin	gypsy
gently legend	register rigid	energy
German stage	magic engine	Egypt

Exceptions to the rule: get gift give girl begins. All have a hard 'g'.
REMEMBER: We must **get** a **gift** to **give** the **gi**rl when she **begi**ns her course.

Magic matching

▶ Draw a line from the description to the word which means the same thing.

Huge	engine
An officer in the army	magic
The name of a country	ginger
Where actors perform	gigantic
Part of a car	gym
When a rabbit jumps from a hat	Egypt
A spice	stage
A place to play ball	general

Alpha to Omega Activity Pack One Plus   © Heinemann Educational 1997

Tracking for 'g': saying /g/ or /j/ — 51

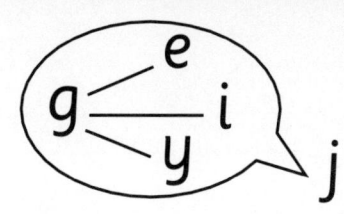

A **gr**inning **gi**ant

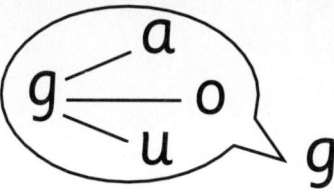

Highlight in a colour the words below that contain a /j/ sound.
Highlight in another colour the words below that contain a /g/ sound.
Beware of the exceptions!

girl general gentle grow gloss large gap gift giant gem page
lag bag hinge glass grass bulge charge engine stagger begin
gin begun binge stage stag gym judge genius genie gum
enlarge gob magic rigid energy humbug got grin gash danger
stranger get give gull ginger gymnast granny glad rigid register

Fill 'em ups

Read the sentences below. Fill in the gaps with either a 'g' or a 'j'. Write the completed sentence on the line below.

1 The __olly green __iant has __in__er hair.

2 He __umped over nine __ars of __am.

3 The __ymnast __umped from the sta__e, full of ener__y.

4 The __udge is going to E__ypt in __anuary.

5 __entle __eorge eats so much fud__e that he is bul__ing.

© Heinemann Educational 1997   Alpha to Omega Activity Pack One Plus

52 Fill the golden jar with gems

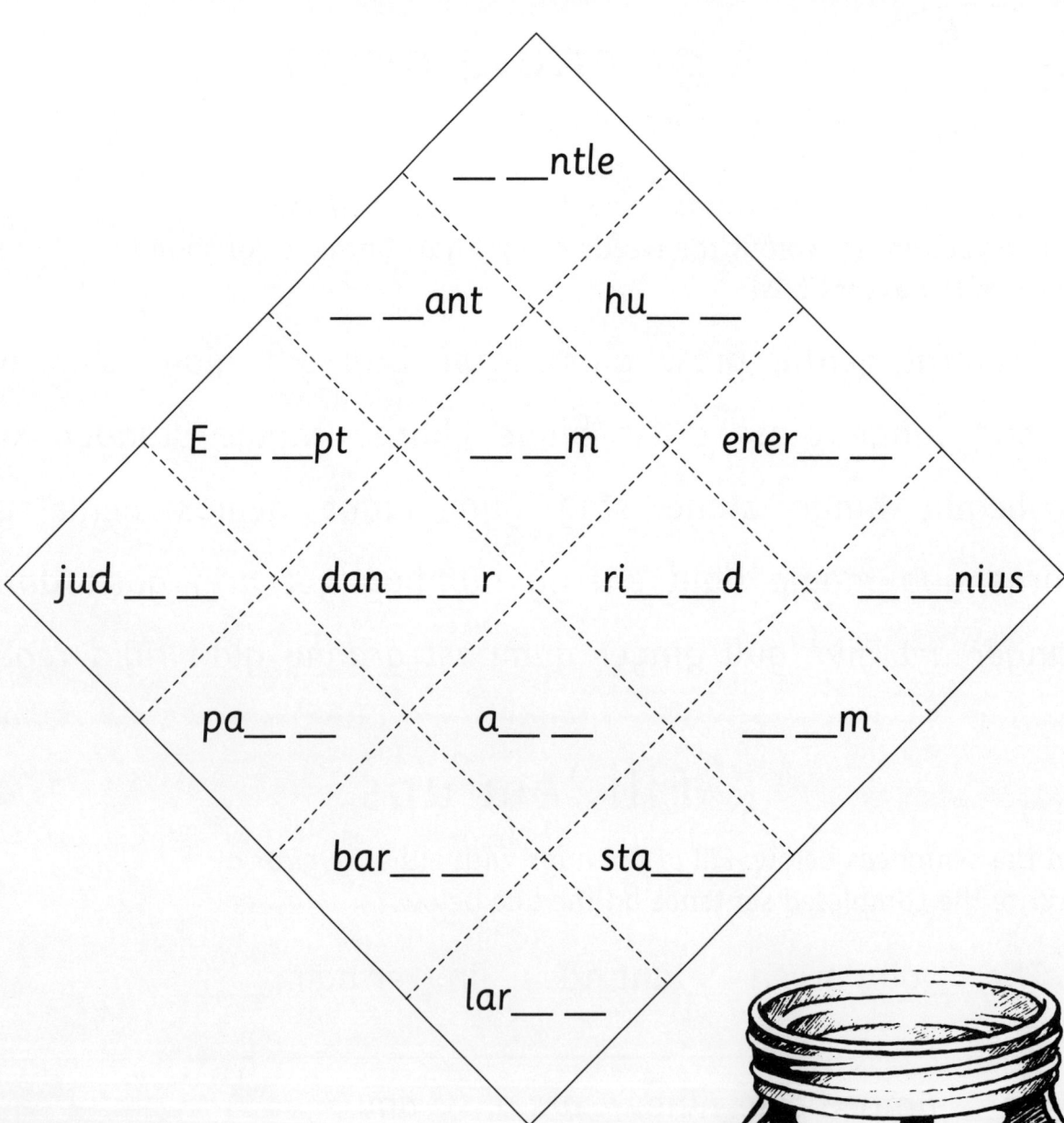

```
        __ __ntle

    __ __ant     hu__ __

  E __ __pt   __ __m    ener__ __

jud __ __  dan__ __r  ri__ __d  __ __nius

    pa__ __    a__ __    __ __m

        bar__ __   sta__ __

              lar__ __
```

Rules: Each player turns over a card, reads the word correctly with a soft 'g' spelling and writes the word correctly in his/her exercise book. The player then puts the card on the jar. If s/he is wrong at any stage the card goes back to the bottom of the pile. The player who has the most words on the jar within 5 minutes wins.

Alpha to Omega Activity Pack One Plus © Heinemann Educational 1997

'o' saying /u/

The loving dove

▶ Read the words below. Colour in the 'o' pattern in each word.

d*o*ve   br*o*ther   n*o*thing   ab*o*ve   *o*ven
s*o*mething   t*o*n   gl*o*ve   fr*o*nt   an*o*ther
L*o*nd*o*n   w*o*nder   n*o*ne   s*o*metimes

▶ Use the words above to fill in the sentences below.
Then underline the /u/ sound. Copy the completed sentences into your exercise book.

1 The _____ flew high _____ the house.

2 My _____ and I shop in _____.

3 There is an _____ in the kitchen.

4 I _____ if I won _____ or nothing in the contest.

5 _____ of my songs was chosen by the D.J.

6 Tom must sit in the _____ row to see well.

7 She looked for _____ map in the _____ box in the car.

8 There is _____ left to eat in the fridge.

© Heinemann Educational 1997   Alpha to Omega Activity Pack One Plus

54 'u' as a wall proofreading

▶ Correct the mis-spellings in this passage. Copy it correctly onto the lines provided.

The Guirl Gides were going to there headquarters were they have a large gest house. They had a vage plan for seeing the sights of London. The gide who wanted to buy a gitar was plaged by roge salesmen who wanted her to perform in the street. She knew that it was in voge to busk, but she also new that this was not allowed. She told the gy who was pushing her the most that he wold be gilty if she called the police.

_____
_____
_____
_____
_____
_____
_____
_____
_____
_____

Alpha to Omega Activity Pack One Plus © Heinemann Educational 1997

'd' as a wall to keep the vowel short 1 — 55

Fill 'em ups

▶ Complete the words in the paragraph below using the 'dge' words provided. Read the completed story.

**trudged judge edge midget bridge sludge
dodging badge ridge hedge**

The j _ _ _ _ said the m _ _ _ _ _, a man of little size, had won a b _ _ _ _ because he had chased the thief d _ _ _ _ _ _ the police. They ran over the b _ _ _ _ _ _, under the h _ _ _ _, around the e _ _ _ of the park, up the hill and across the r _ _ _ _ at the top. Tired out, they t _ _ _ _ _ _ _ through the s _ _ _ _ _ _ only to come face to face with the police.

Proofreading

▶ Correct all the errors in the story below. Write your corrected version into your exercise book.

"May I have a wege of that fuge cake?" asked the loger. The girl nuged her brotha and whispered, "No wonder he is such a poge."

He stirred his tea and replied, "Don't be such a squirt! Can't you see you have hirt his feelings?" The loger's face whent red as he continued to munch his cake.

56 'd' as a wall to keep the vowel short 2

Multiple choice poem

▶ Choose the correct spelling for the missing word and write it in the space provided.

trujed   truged   trudged

We _____ through the snow,

sledge   sleje   slege

With our _____ in tow,

lege   ledge   leje

Until we reached the _____.

ridge   rije   rige

We sat on the _____,

brije   brige   bridge

Next to the _____,

ej   edge   ege

Waiting to move to the _____.

Soon we were sliding down the hill

Dodging   Doging   Dojing

_____ the others, not taking a spill.

baje   bage   badge   **juge   judge   juje**

A _____ was awarded by the _____

We had not a mark

Landing well in the park.

sludge   sluje   sluge

Then back to the top through the _____.

Alpha to Omega Activity Pack One Plus   © Heinemann Educational 1997

't' as a wall for no reason at all! 1

Fill 'em ups poem

Use 'tch' and 'ch' to complete the words below. Then read the poem. Can you find the one exception?

We came back from the ma_____.
Found the door on the la_____.
There wasn't a scra_____ in the ki_____en.
We looked through the ha_____,
And saw a great pa_____
Of ke_____up and mess spread within.
It was su_____ a sight.
We turned off the light
And ran outside to ca_____ it.
It was dark as pi_____.
We looked in the di_____,
And soon found the wre_____ who did it.

© Heinemann Educational 1997

Alpha to Omega Activity Pack One Plus

58 't' as a wall for no reason at all! 2

Proofreading

▶ Correct the story below. Write the corrected story on the lines provided.

The children where sent to gather a basket of eggs whitch the chickens had just laid. They wached as one of the eggs hachd. Cluching their eggs, they ran to the kichen to tell their mother whot they had seen. Mother went back with them to the chicken huch and skechd while we wached the chickens scraching in the cabbage pach. It was a bewiching scene in this wreched part of the world.

_____
_____
_____
_____
_____
_____
_____
_____
_____
_____

Alpha to Omega Activity Pack One Plus © Heinemann Educational 1997

a e i o u are vowels

Vowels say a long sound which is their name

$$\bar{a} \quad b\bar{e} \quad \bar{i} \quad n\bar{o} \quad \bar{u}se$$

or their short sound

$$b\breve{a}t \quad b\breve{e}t \quad \breve{i}t \quad n\breve{o}t \quad \breve{u}p$$

The macron (¯) indicates the long sound.

wāve

A breve (˘) indicates the short sound.

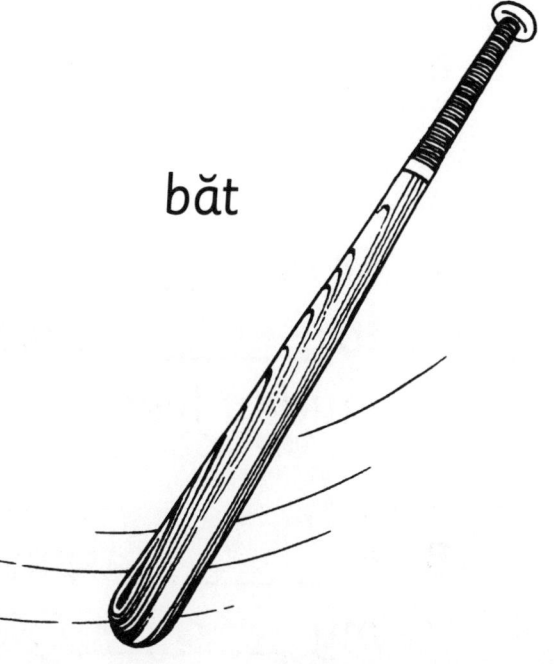

băt

60 Long and short vowel fill 'em ups

Fill in the spaces with the correct word from the list on the left.

mane
man

1 The _____ stroked the _____ of the gentle horse.

cap
cape

2 Ken's vivid silk _____ matches his long striped silk _____.

scrap
scrape
scrapes
scraps
plate
plat

3 Tom had to _____ the _____ of food from the _____ before he did the washing up.

tap
tape
stop
stope

4 Bill put _____ around the hot _____ to _____ it from dripping.

lack
lake

5 The _____ of rain last winter caused the _____ to dry up.

Same
Sam
sam
same

6 _____ saw the _____ film twice.

mat
mate
us
use
wip
wipe

7 Fran's _____ has a mat for _____ to _____ when we _____ our muddy feet.

can
cane
tip
tipe

8 I _____ spin a tin on the _____ of my _____.

Alpha to Omega Activity Pack One Plus © Heinemann Educational 1997

Double or not 1

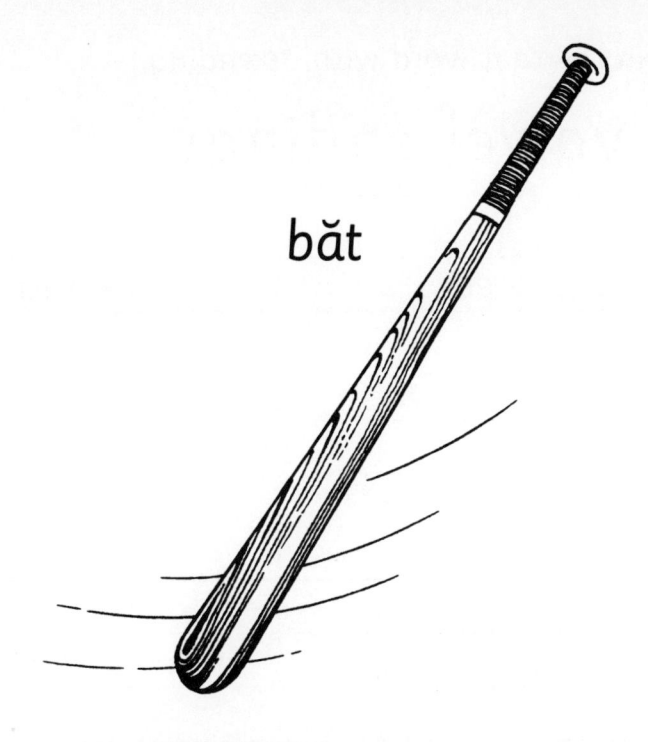

61

băt

A breve (˘) indicates the short sound

root word

| consonant or consonant blends **c** | short vowel **˘v** | consonant **c** |

For example: b a t

+	vowel ending
	ed | ing | er | est

=

| consonant or consonant blends **c** | short vowel **˘v** | consonant **c** | consonant **c** | vowel ending |

© Heinemann Educational 1997   Alpha to Omega Activity Pack One Plus

Double or not 2

▶ Complete the lists below. Write in the root word with its ending.

cvc + vowel endings

Verbs Root word	+ ed	+ ing
hop		
spin		
spot		
slip		
snap		
plan		
scrub		
chop		

Adjectives Root word	+ er	+ est
big		
wet		

cvcc + vowel endings

Verbs Root word	+ ed	+ ing
last		
plant		
work		
rest		
splash		
act		
help		
crunch		
jump		

Adjectives Root word	+ er	+ est
rich		
fast		

Double or not 3

▶ Complete the lists below. Write in the root word with its ending.

cvc and cvcc + vowel endings

Verbs Root word	+ ed	+ ing
pop		
hum		
ask		
end		
stop		
add		
drop		
land		
scrap		
start		
hint		

Adjectives Root word	+ er	+ est
fat		
grand		
thin		

Fill 'em ups

Sam hop__ed over the puddle. It was the wet__est day he had ever seen. He jumped over the next puddle. He splashed in the mud. The mud landed on his cat in the gut__er. He was splashing too. Soon the rain stop__ed. They hur__ied home covered in mud.

Magic 'e'

The long vowel says its name

▶ Read the words below. Put the words with a short vowel sound in the column with the ˘ (breve). Put the words with a long vowel sound in the column with the ˉ (macron). Then put a breve or macron over the short or long vowel in each word and say the word.

cage	bet	bite	scrap	fled
bag	bit	not	scrape	step
tune	kite	note	rate	hop
hug	cod	rip	blend	hope
huge	code	ripe	man	mane

ă ĕ ĭ ŏ ŭ	ā ē ī ō ū

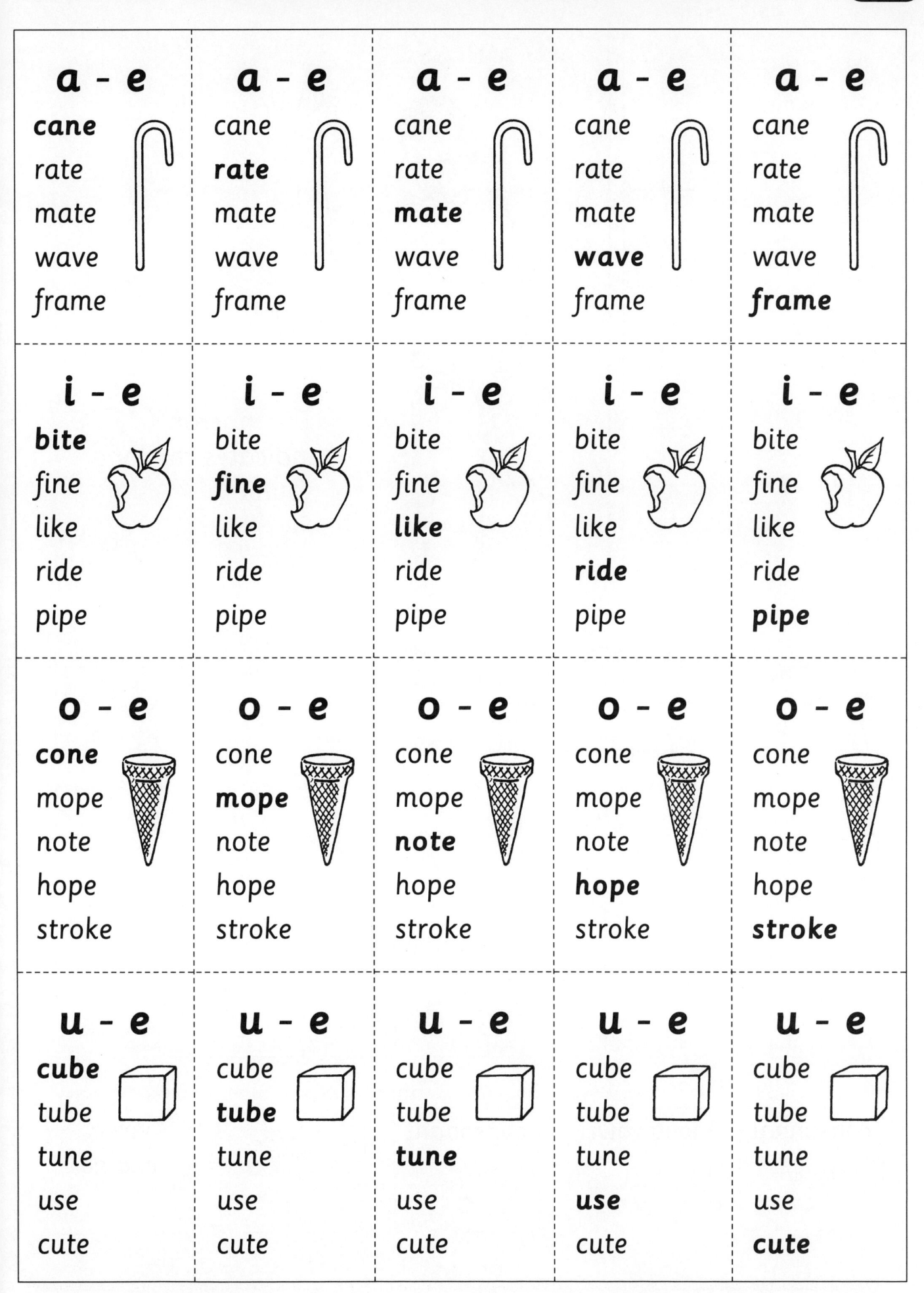

Long vowel families game 65

a - e	a - e	a - e	a - e	a - e
cane	cane	cane	cane	cane
rate	**rate**	rate	rate	rate
mate	mate	**mate**	mate	mate
wave	wave	wave	**wave**	wave
frame	frame	frame	frame	**frame**

i - e	i - e	i - e	i - e	i - e
bite	bite	bite	bite	bite
fine	**fine**	fine	fine	fine
like	like	**like**	like	like
ride	ride	ride	**ride**	ride
pipe	pipe	pipe	pipe	**pipe**

o - e	o - e	o - e	o - e	o - e
cone	cone	cone	cone	cone
mope	**mope**	mope	mope	mope
note	note	**note**	note	note
hope	hope	hope	**hope**	hope
stroke	stroke	stroke	stroke	**stroke**

u - e	u - e	u - e	u - e	u - e
cube	cube	cube	cube	cube
tube	**tube**	tube	tube	tube
tune	tune	**tune**	tune	tune
use	use	use	**use**	use
cute	cute	cute	cute	**cute**

© Heinemann Educational 1997

Alpha to Omega Activity Pack One Plus

66 Drop the silent 'e' 1

wāve

The macron (¯) indicates the long sound

root word

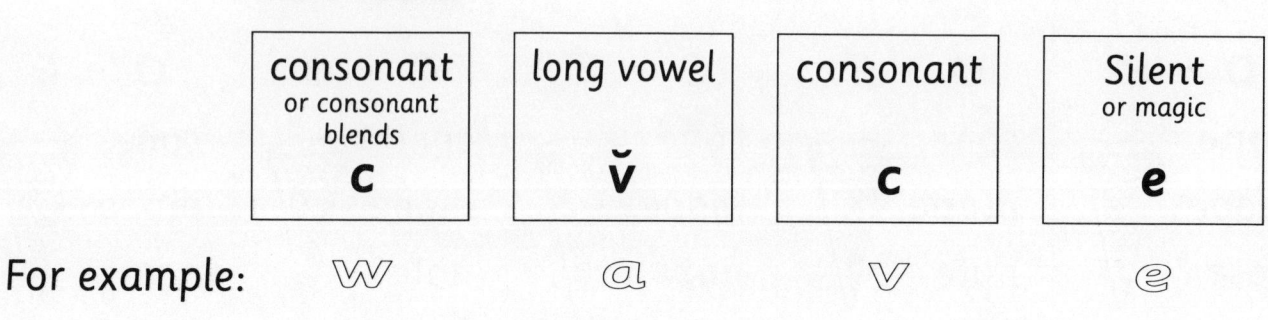

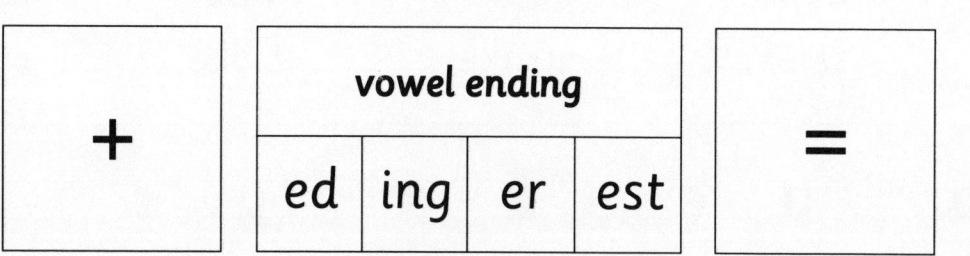

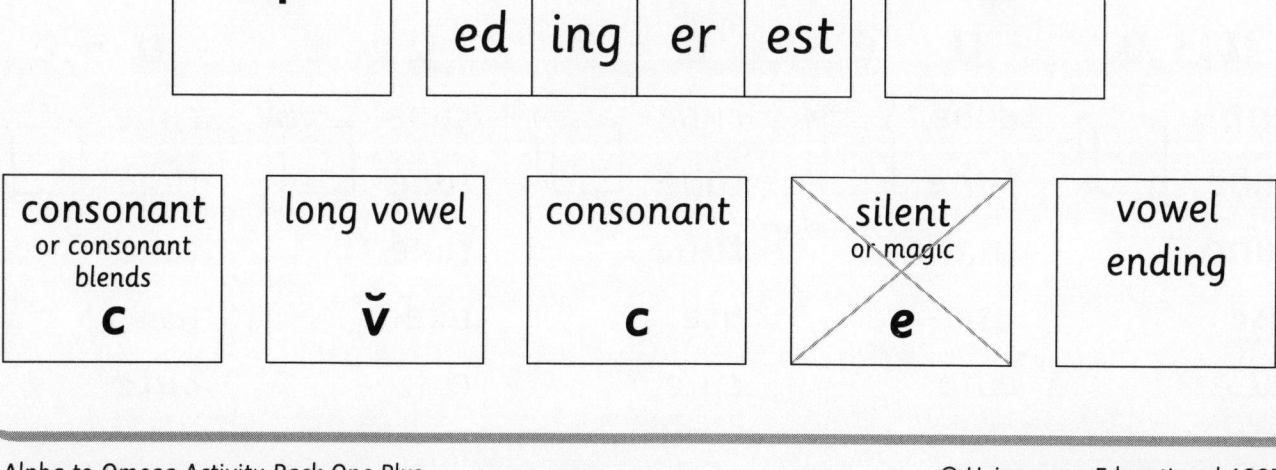

| consonant
or consonant blends
c | long vowel
v̆ | consonant
c | Silent
or magic
e |

For example: w a v e

| + | **vowel ending**
ed \| ing \| er \| est | = |

| consonant
or consonant blends
c | long vowel
v̆ | consonant
c | ~~silent
or magic
e~~ | vowel
ending |

Alpha to Omega Activity Pack One Plus © Heinemann Educational 1997

Drop the silent 'e' 2

cvc'e' + vowel endings

▶ Complete the lists below. Write in the root word with its ending.

Verbs Root word	+ ed	+ ing
hope		
use		
take	————	
rule		
race		
place		
save		
share		
solve		
brake		
smoke		
wave		
serve		
ride		
charge		
force		
taste		
slide	————	
slope		
rhyme		
code		
line		

Adjectives Root word	+ er	+ est
fine		
wide		
late		

© Heinemann Educational 1997 — Alpha to Omega Activity Pack One Plus

Double, drop or not

cvc, cvcc, cvvc and cvc'e' + vowel endings

▶ Complete the lists below. Write in the root word with its ending.

Root word	+ er	+ ing
drop		
camp		
clean		
skate		
clip		
treat		
grin		
dive		
limp		
crave		
tramp		
trap		
scream		

Proofreading

▶ Read the passage below. Correct the mistakes and write the corrected paragraph in your exercise book.

The lad came runing down the street. He loocked at me and screammed, "Go away!" I jumpped up and chassed him. I racked after him and clearred the hedge. Soon we landded and headded for the police station. He shoutted and walcked inside.

Long vowel sound – short vowel spelling

Word search

Find the words listed below in the grid. They go from left to right and top to bottom only. Be sure to read all the words and highlight them carefully when you find them. It helps to cross off the words in the list as you find them.

bind	pint	bolt	old	host	both
blind		colt	bold	most	
grind	child	jolt	cold	almost	yolk
find	mild		fold	post	folk
hind	wild		enfold		
behind			gold		
kind			golden		
mind			hold		
rind			sold		
wind			scold		
			told		

```
i h f e x z b o l t r k m i v e c g
d z q s k d o s f x i s c o l d o m
q c v u m j v o a b n o s d j q l h
u d a p y n q m p h d q z h p f d r
h w l h e w x m p j r x h o l d c c
g o m g n t b o b l i n d u s h j h
o p o r y o l k h t b w u j o l t i
l b s i i p p i n t m o s t c o z l
d f t n a g o l d e n p h b e q d d
u o a d h a w e b g a a o i l b b s
o l d n s q j z o t x r s n k o k t
t d b p c o l t t f x u t d s l m z
r y g s o l d k h e k n u r x d i g
f e n f o l d j v w i l d u t m n d
i g p h i n d y b v n f o l k l d w
n p o s t k h t o l d n n s x e v i
d v f d b e h i n d h s f n h o h n
r e p u a d p z o d m i l d o g m d
```

© Heinemann Educational 1997

Alpha to Omega Activity Pack One Plus

70 Odd words

Find the right word from the list to complete each sentence. Write it in the puzzle. The sentence down the middle will tell you how well you have done.

said   friend   are   were   very   more
forward   they   become   sign   something   bush   England
anything   o'clock   four   gone   whose   sure

1 I can do _____ better than you.
2 "Please, sir, can I have some ____?"
3 It takes ____ to make a quartet.

4 She ____, "Please come home now!"
5 You are ____ good at this.
6 Where ____ you last night?

7 We ___ going for a walk now.

8 He will be ____ when you come back.
9 The line of people crept _____ slowly.
10 Here is _____ for you to do.
11 _____ is a green and pleasant land.
12 On their way home, ____ stopped to chat

13 These are mine, but _____ are these?
14 Are you ____ you know how to do this?
15 The time now is ten _'_____.
16 You will _____ a star in your new show.
17 My best _____ lives very far away.
18 A bird in the hand is worth two in the _____.
19 The ____ over the door says "EXIT".

Alpha to Omega Activity Pack One Plus © Heinemann Educational 1997

Past tense ← present tense → future tense

▲ Fill in the spaces with the correct form of the verb which is given in front of each of the following sentences. Remember, a verb is a doing word.

be   **1** I *was* hungry an hour ago. | I *am* hungry right now. | I *will be* hungry in an hour.

play **2** Last year I _____ the trumpet. | This year I _____ the drums. | Next year I _____ the piano.

go   **3** I _____ to school when I was five. | I _____ to school every day. | I _____ to a new school soon.

eat   **4** I _____ peas when I was little. | I _____ peas now. | I _____ peas when I am older.

wake **5** I _____ up early yesterday. | I _____ up early every day. | I _____ up early in summer.

water **6** I _____ the plants yesterday. | I _____ the plants every day. | I _____ the plants tomorrow.

cycle **7** I _____ to Pat's last week. | I _____ to Pat's every day. | I _____ to Pat's tomorrow.

read **8** I _____ books when I was four. | I _____ books now. | I _____ books when I am fifty.

bloom **9** The roses _____ last month. | The roses _____ every year. | The roses _____ in June.

Verbs 1

▶ Read the following sentences and underline the verb, or 'doing' word. Then put the sentence into the **past tense**.

1. I <u>will finish</u> my work before everyone else.

   I finished my work before everyone else.

2. She will help cut the grass this weekend.

   _____

3. I often take long walks in the forest.

   _____

4. I play football every Thursday and watch cricket on Mondays.

   _____

   _____

5. Mark will sing at the concert.

   _____

6. She opens her presents very quickly.

   _____

▶ Underline the verb or verbs in each of the following sentences. Then put each sentence into the **present tense**.

1. I <u>will help</u> Dad <u>mend</u> the chair.

   I help Dad mend the chair.

2. Chicken soup with rice will make a nice meal.

   _____

3. I fed my goldfish every morning before school.

   _____

continued on sheet 73

Alpha to Omega Activity Pack One Plus © Heinemann Educational 1997

Verbs 2

continued from sheet 72

4 Jack and Alex used to skate every day.

_____

5 We took the train when it was raining.

_____

6 I wore my helmet when riding.

_____

Read the following sentences and underline the verb.
Then put each sentence into the **future tense**.

1 I <u>woke</u> up early yesterday.

    I will wake up early tomorrow.

2 I went to the cinema last Saturday.

_____

3 Peter picked a sack of peppers.

_____

4 Maggie is painting her room.

_____

5 I am helping my sister.

_____

6 Bill and Ted ran around the block.

_____

© Heinemann Educational 1997   Alpha to Omega Activity Pack One Plus

Nouns 1

Articles

▶ Read the story below. Fill in the blanks with either 'a' or 'an'.

I need ____ blue marking pen to finish my project and Sarah needs ____ orange one. It is ____ interesting project given to us by ____ teacher's assistant. Before we begin, however, I must eat ____ sandwich for lunch. It is on ____ very tasty bap and has ____ bit of lettuce, ____ bit of tomato and ____ huge slice of cheddar in it. I also have ____ apple and ____ bottle of water. Sarah has ____ brown bag with her lunch in it, tied up with ____ old piece of string.

When we have finished eating, we will find ____ quiet place to work. I must write about ____ ape I saw on ____ outing to ____ nearby zoo and Sarah must draw ____ picture of ____ ugly baboon she saw swinging from ____ vine.

Plural nouns

▶ Write the plural form of each noun below in the blank space provided.

one man	two _____
one bush	five _____
one penny	three _____
one toy	six _____
one ship	nine _____
one house	seven _____
one football team	twelve football _____

Alpha to Omega Activity Pack One Plus © Heinemann Educational 1997

Nouns 2

Proper nouns and common nouns

▶ Read the following paragraph. Underline the proper nouns. Circle the common nouns.

My best (friend) is named <u>Jack</u>. We live in the city of London, which is in England. England is part of Europe even though it is an island. Jack has a brother named Max. I have a sister named Sam. All of us were born in June, and every year we celebrate together. Sometimes Jack has a party on the first Saturday in June. I have a party on the second Saturday in June. Max has a party on the third Saturday in June, and Sam has her party on the last Saturday in June.

Pronouns

▶ Read the sentences below. Replace the proper noun or nouns in each sentence with one of these pronouns:

he   they   it   she   them   him

1 Dad likes to make pots. _He likes to make pots._

2 Bart and Lisa are friends. _____

3 Bath is a nice city to visit. _____

4 Mum called Meg and Maggie to dinner. _____

5 Mr Smith wants Karen to help him. _____

© Heinemann Educational 1997   Alpha to Omega Activity Pack One Plus

76 Apostrophe

The little mark with the big job

▶ Read the sentences below. Then write them out so there are no more apostrophes.

1 Penny's best friend is Sasha.

   The best friend of Penny is Sasha.

2 Sasha's best friend is Penny.

3 Sasha borrows Penny's pencil.

4 It's her green pencil with the dull tip.

▶ Correct the following sentences. Insert apostrophes where necessary.

1 Sasha breaks the pencils tip.

2 She doesnt usually have a problem.

3 Pennys happy to help but cant sharpen it either.

4 The sharpener wont work properly.

Alpha to Omega Activity Pack One Plus   © Heinemann Educational 1997

Questions?

who   what   when   where   why   how   which   whose

▶ Read the sentences below. In each sentence circle the word that turns it into a question.

1. What is the best way to travel to France?
2. Where did you leave the basket?
3. Why do we turn clocks forward in the spring?
4. When does the film begin?
5. How long will it take to get to your house if we run all the way?
6. Who can connect my computer to the Internet?
7. Which game do you like better?
8. Whose pencil case is this?

▶ Fill in the sentences below with one of the question words at the top of the page. Do not use the same word more than once.

1. _____ are you doing after school?
2. _____ can Auntie Roz come to visit us?
3. _____ many ghosts did you see last night?
4. _____ did your cute little black and white puppy go?
5. _____ do these berries cost so much?
6. _____ of these films shall we see?
7. _____ is Prime Minister now?
8. _____ pencil is dark blue?

© Heinemann Educational 1997   Alpha to Omega Activity Pack One Plus

78 Yes or no questions

▶ Read the following sentences. Change the order of the words in each sentence to create a question which must be answered by yes or no.

1 The bird is sitting on the branch.

   Is the bird sitting on the branch?

2 Fred is cycling to the park.

   _____

3 The cow is milked every day.

   _____

4 The earth is circling the sun.

   _____

5 Ted and Rob are having ice cream today.

   _____

▶ Change the order of the words in the following questions to make a statement.

1 Was Robin Hood a hero?

   Robin Hood was a hero.

2 Is the weather good for sailing today?

   _____

3 Are there nice oranges in the shop?

   _____

4 Are you walking home from school today?

   _____

Alpha to Omega Activity Pack One Plus © Heinemann Educational 1997

Intonation

79

▶ Read the questions below and see how the meaning changes depending on which word is emphasised.

Did Jan wash this jumper?
Did **Jan** wash this jumper?
Did Jan **wash** this jumper?
Did Jan wash **this** jumper?
Did Jan wash this **jumper**?

▶ Read the sentence below. Write it out three times in your exercise book. In each sentence underline a different word that can change the meaning of the sentence if that word is emphasised.

Did Ted borrow my pen?

▶ Now write a question of your own that can have several meanings depending on how it is asked. Write it out at least three times to show at least three different meanings by underlining the important words.

1 _____

2 _____

3 _____

4 _____

© Heinemann Educational 1997

Alpha to Omega Activity Pack One Plus

80 Busy, dizzy commas

▶ Read the poem below.

> Annie Sammy Johnny and Joan
> Went to London New York and Rome.
> They travelled by ferry car and train
> By sledge bus cycle and plane.
>
> They danced skipped shouted and raved.
> They walked ran skated and waved.
> They exclaimed screamed and laughed out loud.
> They stared explored and got lost in the crowd.
>
> The large bulky ferry dropped them in Dover.
> Their wonderful splendid trip was over.
> The suntanned happy smiling four
> Were excited delighted and ready for more.

▶ Underline the nouns in the first verse with a colour.
▶ Underline the verbs in the second verse with a different colour.
▶ Underline the adjectives in the third verse with another colour.

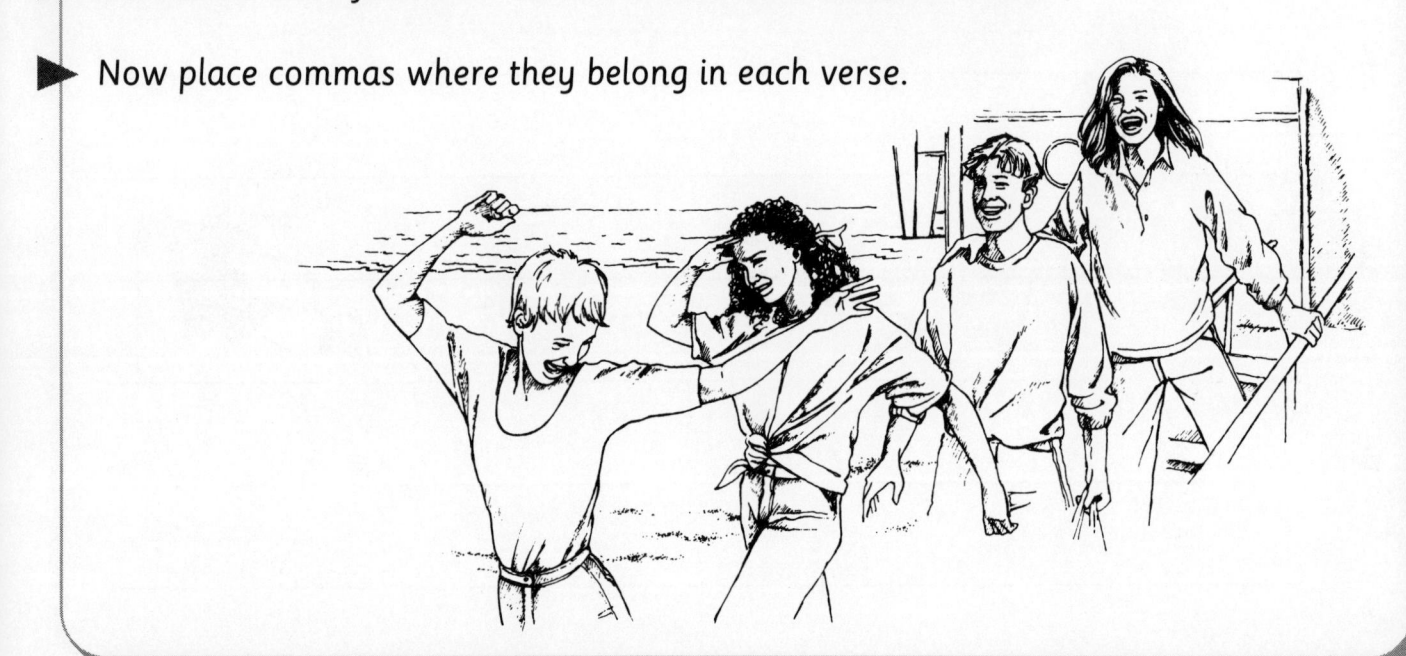

▶ Now place commas where they belong in each verse.

Alpha to Omega Activity Pack One Plus © Heinemann Educational 1997

Commas and speech marks

▶ Read the story below and put in the commas and speech marks. Copy the corrected text into your exercise book.

Johnny, let's go on a trip! said his friends Annie Sammy and Joan. Where are we going? he asked. I'll have to ask my mum. Well, we could get a bus to take us to London. Oh, that's no fun! Let's ride our bikes! screamed Sammy. I want to take the train and a ferry shouted Annie. Let's go to Rome! I've been there Joan exclaimed. I want to take a plane to New York. The girls argued fussed and moaned while Johnny went off to ask his mother. You can go she said but only in the new way. What's that? asked Johnny. You can all go down to the cyber cafe in town. Ask them for a virtual reality world tour. Then you can go wherever you want and get there however you want and you can be home in time for tea. Johnny went and told his friends. They laughed out loud and shouted What a great idea. They couldn't wait to get there.

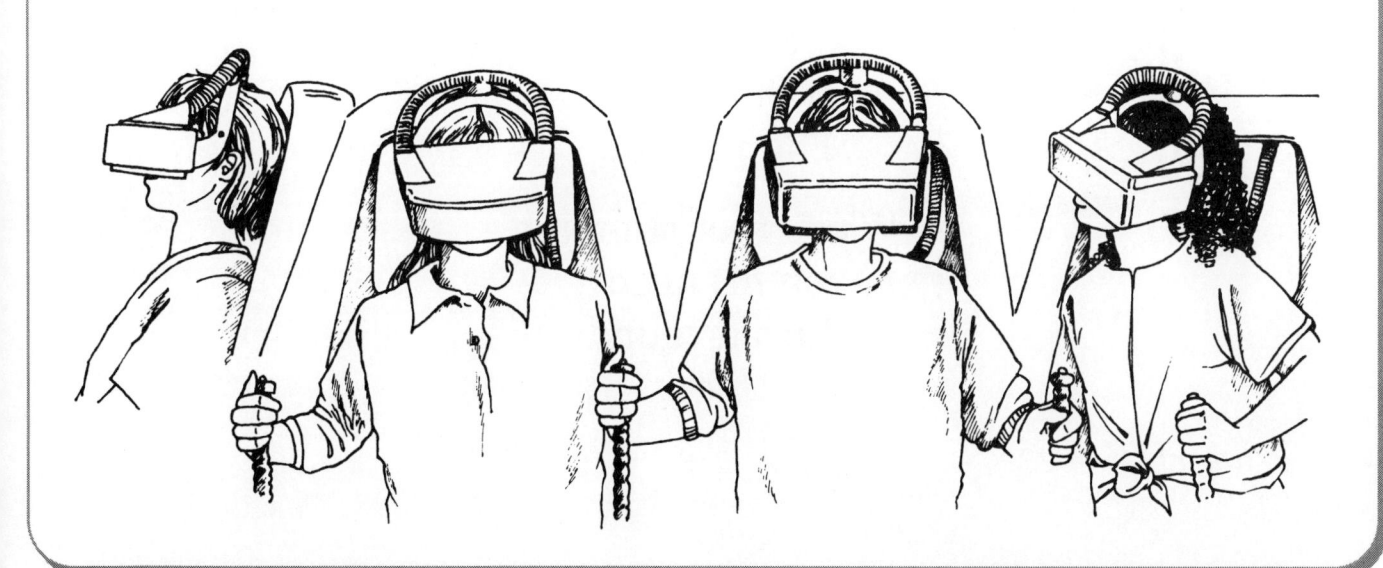

© Heinemann Educational 1997 Alpha to Omega Activity Pack One Plus

Ready for rhyming 1

▶ Read the poem below and highlight the words that rhyme.

Going through the old photos
by Michael Rosen

Who's that?
That's your Auntie Mabel
and that's me
under the table.

Who's that?
That's Uncle Billy.
Who's that?
Me being silly.

Who's that
licking a lolly?
I'm not sure
but I think it's Polly.

Who's that
behind the tree?
I don't know,
I can't see.
Could be you.
Could be me.

Who's that?
Baby Joe.
Who's that?
I don't know.

Who's that standing
on his head?
Turn it round.
It's Uncle Ted.

▶ Now look at sheet 83.

Ready for rhyming 2

You have read this poem on sheet 82. Fill in the missing words to complete the poem.

Going through the old photos
by Michael Rosen

Who's that?
That's your Auntie _____
and that's me
under the _____.

Who's that?
That's Uncle _____.
Who's that?
Me being _____.

Who's that
licking a _____?
I'm not sure
but I think it's _____.

Who's that
behind the _____?
I don't know,
I can't see.
Could be you.
Could be _____.

Who's that?
Baby _____.
Who's that?
I don't _____.

Who's that standing
on his _____?
Turn it round.
It's Uncle _____.

© Heinemann Educational 1997

Alpha to Omega Activity Pack One Plus

Sequencing

84

Put the pictures in order; then match the sentences to the pictures.

How to cook spaghetti

When the spaghetti is done, pour a cup of cold water into the pot.

Drain the spaghetti and serve.

In a large pot, bring lots of cold water to the boil.

When the water is boiling, add the spaghetti.

Stir the spaghetti with a fork.

Alpha to Omega Activity Pack One Plus © Heinemann Educational 1997

Sentence sequencing

Treasure Island
by Robert Louis Stevenson
(adapted by Lisa Norby)

▶ Jim is a young cabin boy on a ship called the **Hispaniola**. The ship has landed at Treasure Island. There are pirates amongst the crew and Jim is not very friendly with them. The pirates want to find the gold and abandon Jim and the captain. Jim has a plan. Put the sentences in order to find out what it is.

This was my plan.

1. The ship would drift in to shore and get stuck in the sand.
2. But for now the pirates could not sail away and leave us marooned.
3. I would cut the **Hispaniola** loose from its anchor.
4. Later we could pull it free.

▶ Write your order here: _____, _____, _____, _____

▶ Now write the sentences as a paragraph.

This was my plan. _____

_____

_____

_____

_____

© Heinemann Educational 1997   Alpha to Omega Activity Pack One Plus

Paragraph sequencing

Kidnapped
by Robert Louis Stevenson
(adapted by Lisa Norby)

▶ Cut out the paragraphs and put them in the correct order.

David is on board the sailing ship **Covenant**. It has just sailed through a storm.

An hour later, I was cast up onto a small island. I had swallowed a good bit of the sea. My legs felt like logs. But I dared not lie down to rest. It was a cold night. In my wet clothes I was in danger of freezing to death. So I walked the shore until dawn.

All at once I understood. I had been roaming the island for four days, but every time I came to the creek it was high tide. Now I waited for the tide to go out. Nothing was left of the creek but a trickle of water. I walked across to the Isle of Mull.

My little island was separated from the larger Isle of Mull by a deep creek. Across the water I could see the smoke from a chimney. But I was no swimmer.

I went down twice. When I came up for the second time, the current had swept me far from the **Covenant**. I grabbed hold of a piece of floating timber and began kicking my way toward the shore.

On the fourth day I saw two fishermen in a boat. I screamed for help. Instead of coming to rescue me, they laughed. One of them shouted at me. I could hardly hear him, but I made out the word "tide".

But at that moment, the tide caught the **Covenant**. The ship spun around like a top. It crashed into a reef with such force that I was knocked off my feet. Seconds later, a huge wave tilted the ship onto her side, and I was thrown into the sea.

For three days I slept in a crude shelter. Small shellfish clung to the rocks along the shore. I picked them off and ate them raw. I was so hungry that they tasted wonderful.

Alpha to Omega Activity Pack One Plus © Heinemann Educational 1997

Comprehension: Oliver Twist 1

Oliver Twist

by Charles Dickens
(adapted by Les Martin)

Oliver Twist was born in a workhouse. His mother died when he was born, so he lived in an orphanage. When he asked for more food to eat, he was sent out of the orphanage to work for an undertaker. He didn't like it there and got into a fight. Then he ran away to London. On his way, he met The Dodger who took him to live and work with Fagin.

During the next few days, Oliver saw how much Fagin cared about his boys.

When they came back with watches, wallets and handkerchiefs, Fagin patted their heads. And gave them extra sausage. But sometimes they came back empty-handed. Then Fagin got angry at them. He sent them to bed without supper.

"Hurts me more than you," he said. "But you must learn not to be lazy."

Oliver saw more of Fagin's kindness when two visitors arrived.

One was a tall man with a bad temper and big muscles. His name was Bill Sikes. The strong young woman with him was called Nancy. She was messy-looking but nice. Oliver liked her.

"Nancy grew up with me," Fagin said. "Now she devotes herself to Bill. Bill makes a fine living as, er, a salesman. And Nancy is all set to be his wife someday."

"Yeah, someday," Nancy said.

"Enough gab," Bill said. "How much for this?" He took silverware and silver candlesticks from his sack.

Fagin dropped a gold piece on the table. Bill's fist made the coin jump. Slowly Fagin let a few copper coins clink down.

continued on sheet 88

Comprehension: Oliver Twist 2

"My limit," Fagin said.

Bill growled. Then he scooped up the money and left with Nancy.

"Lovely couple," Fagin said. "Wish I could help them more. But you boys are such a burden for a poor man."

"I know," said Oliver. "I'd like to do my full share. Please, sir, can I go out to work like the others?"

"A fine boy, a willing boy," said Fagin. He smiled at Oliver fondly.

When the Dodger heard the news, he said, "Knew you had the right stuff, Oliver. Come with me and Charley. We'll start you off right."

Oliver followed them through the streets to a nicer part of London. Well-dressed men and women strolled on clean pavements. The sun was bright. The air was sweet.

The Dodger stopped suddenly. He pointed to a bookstall across the street.

"See that old man with the white hair?" he asked quietly.

"Yes," said Oliver.

"Perfect!" said Charley Bates.

The man was reading a book with great interest. The Dodger and Charley nodded to each other. Oliver saw the Dodger slink up to the gentleman. The Dodger's hand dipped into the gentleman's pocket. It pulled out a handkerchief.

For the first time Oliver knew what the "work" of Fagin's boys really was!

Comprehension: Oliver Twist 3

continued from sheet 88

The bookstall owner shouted, "Stop, thief!"

The Dodger and Charley raced around a corner. Oliver saw only one thing he could do. Run!

Oliver ran right into a good citizen. That good citizen stopped Oliver. With the first thing that came to hand. A fist.

Oliver saw stars. Then blackness. Finally that blackness brightened. Oliver opened his eyes. Yet he was sure he was dreaming.

Either that, or he had died and gone to heaven.

Questions about the characters

1 What sort of work do you think Fagin and his boys do?

_____

_____

_____

2 "Bill makes a fine living as, er, a salesman". Is he really a salesman? What does he do?

_____

_____

3 Fagin says Oliver is "a fine boy, a willing boy". Is Oliver like this? Give your reasons.

_____

_____

_____

_____

continued on sheet 90

© Heinemann Educational 1997   Alpha to Omega Activity Pack One Plus

Comprehension: Oliver Twist 4

continued from sheet 89

Questions about the story

4 Was Fagin a kind man? Give your reasons.

5 Oliver wanted to do his "fair share" of work. What was the work that Fagin's boys did?

6 The Dodger is the leader of Fagin's boys. Where do he and Charley Bates take Oliver? How do they get there?

7 The Dodger and Charley raced around a corner. What happened to Oliver?

Questions about how the story is written

8 Explain, in your own words, what the following mean:

   a "Bill's fist made the coin jump."

continued on sheet 91

Comprehension: Oliver Twist 5

continued from sheet 90

b a good citizen

_____
_____

c Oliver saw stars.

_____
_____

9 Is Fagin a good, honest man? How do you know?

_____
_____
_____

10 When Oliver opened his eyes, he thought he was dreaming or in heaven. Where do you think he was? Continue the story.

_____
_____
_____
_____
_____
_____
_____
_____
_____

continued on sheet 92

Comprehension: Oliver Twist 6

Questions about your opinion

11 Did you like reading this story?

        YES_____ NO_____

Give your reasons.

_____
_____
_____
_____
_____
_____
_____

12 Would you like to find out what happens to Oliver?

_____
_____
_____
_____

13 Would you like to be one of Fagin's boys and girls?

_____
_____
_____
_____

Comprehension: A wedding day in the 1940s 1 — 93

▶ Look at the photograph and read about weddings during the Second World War. Read about Frank and Kitty's wedding.

These people got married during the Second World War.

Sometimes people got married quickly because they had to go back to the fighting or had to do secret work.

The woman is carrying a box and the man is wearing a bag. Inside the box is her gas mask. He has his gas mask in his bag.

Many women did not have wedding dresses. They were very hard to buy. Sometimes women made their dresses from parachute silk.

The church is covered with bags. They are sand bags to stop the church from being damaged by bombs.

continued on sheet 94

© Heinemann Educational 1997　　　Alpha to Omega Activity Pack One Plus

94 Comprehension: A wedding day in the 1940s 2
continued from sheet 93

Frank and Kitty were married during the war, but the marriage almost didn't happen. Frank worked in an iron foundry. He could have a week's holiday. Kitty, however, was trained to decode messages from the enemy. She could be sent anywhere in the country at any time, but she could not say where she was going or what she was doing. Frank and Kitty planned to be married on 22 January, but Kitty had to go away to work. This happened twice more. Frank's mother was beginning to think that Kitty didn't want to marry Frank. Then in June, Kitty got time off and they got married very quickly. Then Kitty had to go back to work. They had their honeymoon after the war was over.

Vocabulary

▶ Match the words to the definitions. Use your dictionary or an encyclopaedia to help you.

Word		Meaning	
1	decode	a	a place where iron is melted and moulded
2	gas mask	b	a light cover with ropes attached used when you jump from a plane to the ground
3	honeymoon	c	to change writing into words you understand
4	iron foundry	d	a strong bag full of sand used to protect buildings
5	parachute	e	a mask which filters air filled with gas
6	sand bag	f	the holiday taken after a wedding

continued on sheet 95

Alpha to Omega Activity Pack One Plus © Heinemann Educational 1997

Comprehension: A wedding day in the 1940s 3 | 95

continued from sheet 94

▶ Now answer these questions.

1. Sometimes people got married quickly in the war. Why did they have to do that?

   _____

   _____

   _____

   _____

2. The woman in the photograph is carrying a box. What is in it?

   _____

   _____

   _____

3. How long did Frank and Kitty have to wait to get married?

   _____

   _____

4. It was often not easy to get married during the war. What made it hard?

   _____

   _____

   _____

   _____

© Heinemann Educational 1997   Alpha to Omega Activity Pack One Plus

96 Words you need to know 1: Exam words

Mix and match

▶ Learn the meanings of the words below. Then cut them up, mix them up and match them up again.

Words	Meanings
comment	say what you think
describe	tell about, make a picture in words
explain	show, make something clear
imagine	pretend
layout	the way words and pictures are put on a page
passage	part of a story or writing
persuade	win someone over by your writing
phrases	groups of words which go together
reasons	say why you think what you do
refer	go back to
support	back up what you have said

Words you need to know 2: Exam words   97

Cloze passage

The instructions below have words missing. The meanings of the missing words are given in brackets after the blank. Write the correct word in the blank.

_____ (**say what you think**) on how the _____ (**the way the words and pictures are put on the page**) helps you to understand the problems people had getting married during the Second World War.

_____ (**make a picture in your own words**) Kitty's job during the war. What does the _____ (**group of words**) 'decode messages' in the _____ (**part of the writing**) mean? Give your _____ (**say why you think what you do**) to _____ (**back up what you have said**) what you have written.

_____ (**go back to**) to the passage about Kitty and Frank and _____ (**show, make clear**) why Kitty had to delay their wedding.

_____ (**pretend**) that you are Frank. How would you _____ (**win over by writing**) your mother that Kitty really wants to marry you?

98 Words you need to know 3: Exam words

Crossword puzzle

Word list
comment   describe
explain   imagine
layout   passage

Word list
persuade   phrases
reasons   refer
support

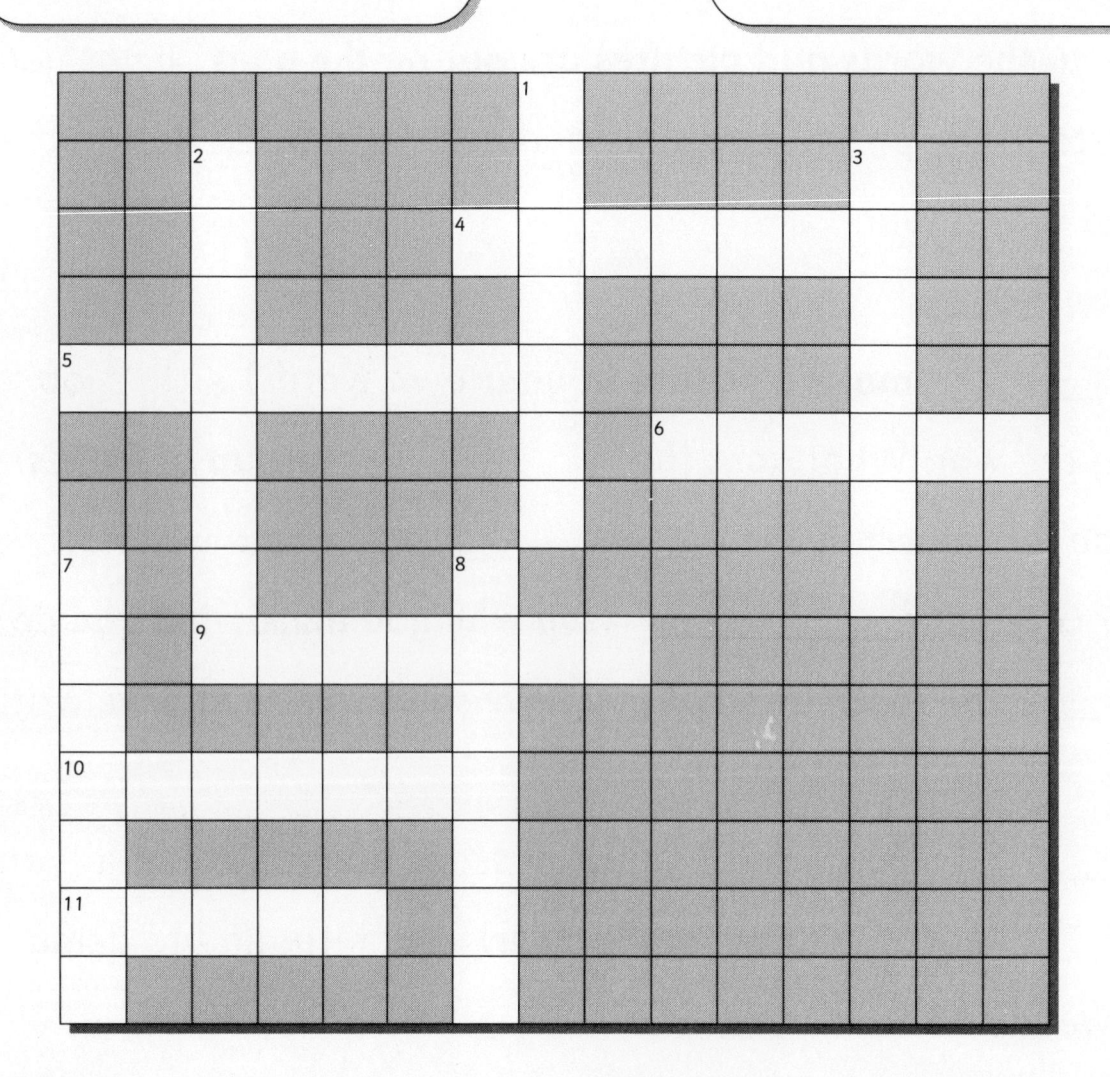

Clues across
4 Pretend
5 Tell about, make a picture in words
6 The way words and pictures are put on a page
9 Show, make something clear
10 Groups of words which go together
11 Go back

Clues down
1 Say what you think
2 Win someone over by your writing
3 Say why you think what you do
7 Back up what you have said
8 Part of a story or writing

Alpha to Omega Activity Pack One Plus © Heinemann Educational 1997

Words you need to know 4: English

Mix and match

▶ Learn the meanings of the words below. Then cut them up, mix them up and match them up again.

Word	Meaning
noun	a word which names someone or something
pronoun	a word which replaces a noun
verb	a word showing action, doing or being
adjective	a word which describes a noun
adverb	a word which describes an adjective, a verb or another adverb
sentence	a group of words which state a complete thought
phrase	a group of words which are part of a sentence
paragraph	a group of sentences expressing a whole part of a story

100 Words you need to know 5: English

Crossword puzzle

Word list
adjective   adverb
noun   paragraph

Word list
phrase   pronoun
sentence   verb

Clues across
1. A group of sentences expressing a whole part of a story or essay, such as the beginning
4. A word which replaces a noun
6. A word showing action, doing or being
7. A word which names someone or something
8. A word which describes a noun

Clues down
2. A word which describes an adjective
3. A group of words which state a complete thought
5. A group of words which are part of a sentence

Alpha to Omega Activity Pack One Plus   © Heinemann Educational 1997

Words you need to know 6: Maths

Mix and match

▶ Learn the meanings of the words below. Then cut them up, mix them up and match them up again.

Word	Meaning
alternate	every other; skip one number, go to the next
consecutive	the very next number
estimating	a guess based on what you know
fractions	parts of a whole, written with number of parts given on the top and the number of parts in the whole on the bottom
decimal	parts of ten written by putting a decimal point (.) after the whole number and followed by the decimal number
add	to make a number larger by joining it with others to make a new total
subtract	to make a number smaller by taking others away from it to make a new total
multiply	to make a number larger by adding it to itself a certain number of times
graph	a chart drawn on squared paper using a line to show change
metre	a measure of length or distance
equilateral	sides of the same length
symmetry	when an object is divided by a line and both parts are the same in size, shape and position
rotate	turn
degree	how angles are measured; it is written with ° after the number

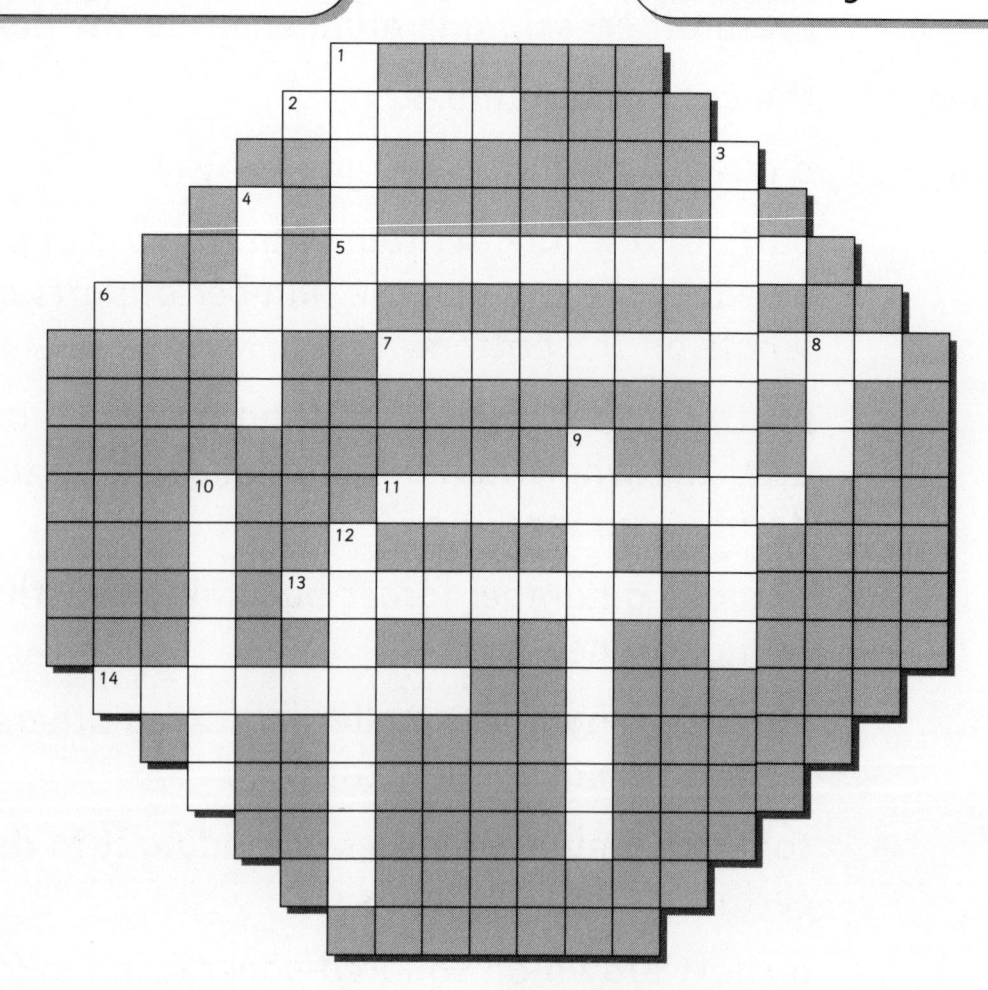

102 Words you need to know 7: Maths

Crossword puzzle

Word list
- fractions
- metre
- rotate
- symmetry
- graph
- multiply
- subtract

Word list
- add
- consecutive
- degree
- estimating
- alternate
- decimal
- equilateral

Clues across
2. A measure of length
5. A guess based on what you know
6. Turn
7. Sides of the same length
11. Every other: skip one number and go to next
13. To make a number smaller by taking others away
14. When an object is divided by a line and both parts are the same in size, shape and position

Clues down
1. How angles are measured
3. The very next number
4. A chart drawn on squared paper using a line to show change
8. To make a number larger
9. Parts of a whole
10. Parts of ten
12. To make a number larger by adding it to itself a certain number of times

Alpha to Omega Activity Pack One Plus © Heinemann Educational 1997

Words you need to know 8: General science

Mix and match

▶ Learn the meanings of the words below. Then cut them up, mix them up and match them up again.

Word	Meaning
absorb	to take in
apparatus	the equipment needed to carry out a scientific experiment
degree	a scale mark on a thermometer
equipment	the things needed to do a job
experiment	a test done to prove or discover facts
machine	a device that uses power to do work
thermometer	instrument for measuring temperature
translucent	lets light through but you cannot see through it
transparent	you can see through it
volume	the space taken up by a thing or person

104 Words you need to know 9: General science

Crossword puzzle

Word list
absorb   apparatus
degree   equipment
experiment

Word list
machine   thermometer
translucent   transparent
volume

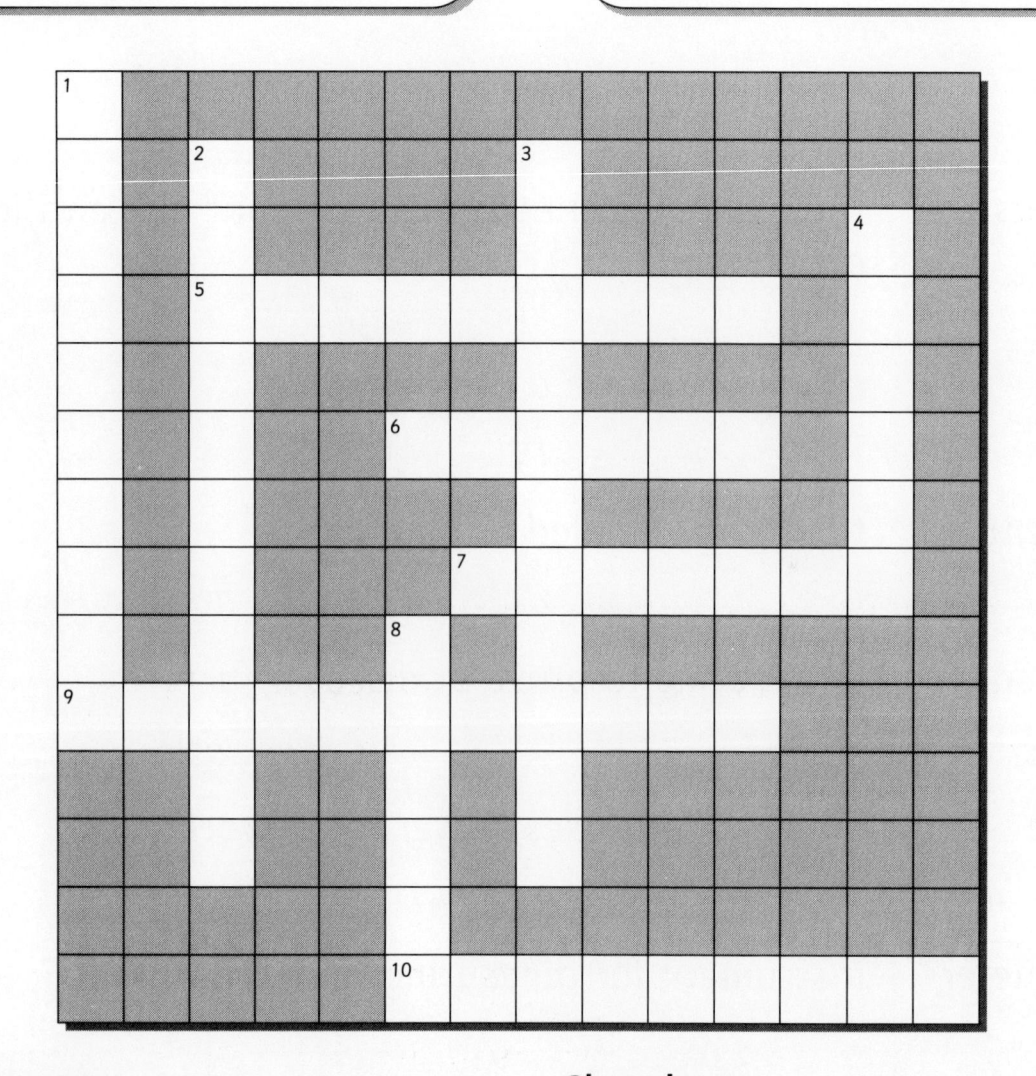

Clues across
5 The equipment needed to carry out a scientific experiment
6 To take in
7 A device that uses power to do work
9 Instrument for measuring temperature
10 The things needed to do a job

Clues down
1 A test done to prove or discover facts
2 Lets light through but you cannot see through it
3 You can see through it
4 A scale mark on a thermometer
8 The space taken up by a thing or person

Alpha to Omega Activity Pack One Plus   © Heinemann Educational 1997

Words you need to know 10: Biology

Mix and match

▶ Learn the meanings of the words below. Then cut them up, mix them up and match them up again.

Word	Meaning
biology	the study of living things
ecology	the study of plants and animals in their environment
ecosystem	group of living things living together
expand	to get bigger, e.g. lungs when you breathe in
growth	an animal or plant getting bigger
habitat	the place where a plant or animal lives
germinate	begin to grow, e.g. as a seed does in warm, damp earth
nutrition	getting food and using it for growth
oxygen	a gas found in air and which all living things use for breathing
reproduction	the process of animals or plants making more of themselves
respiration	breathing
skeleton	the bones in an animal that hold it together
sunlight	natural light that allows green plants to live
temperature	how hot or cold something is

© Heinemann Educational 1997   Alpha to Omega Activity Pack One Plus

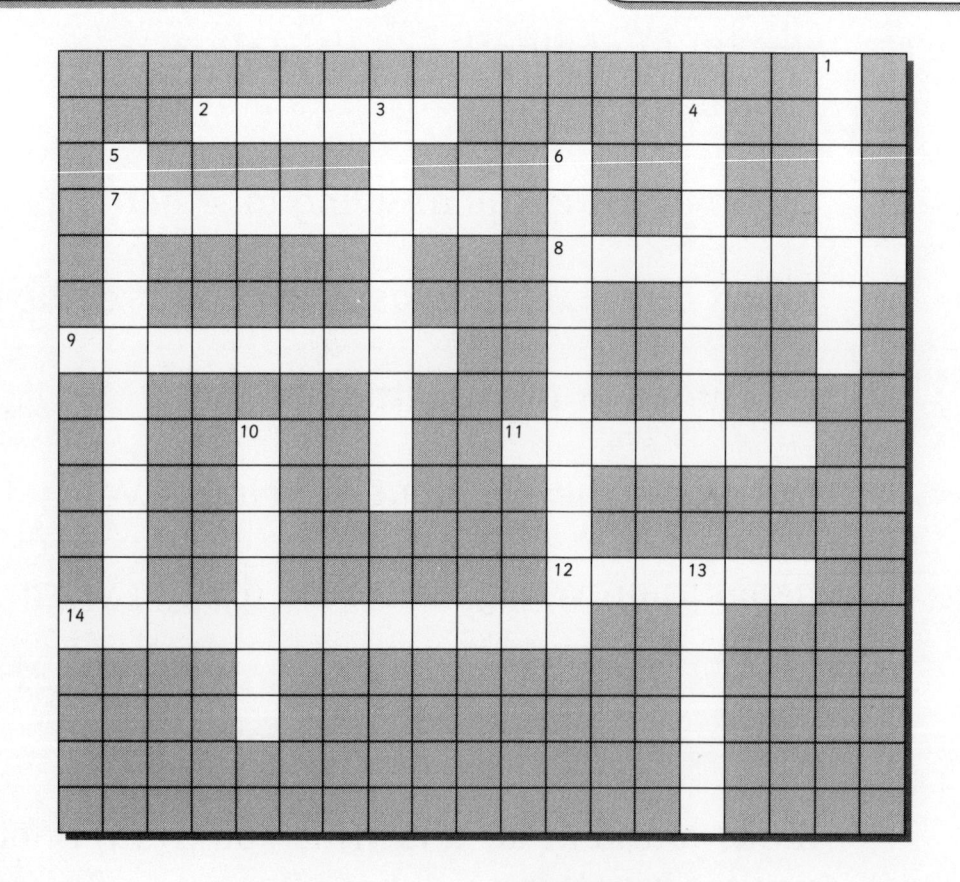

106 Words you need to know 11: Biology

Crossword puzzle

Word list
- biology
- ecosystem
- germinate
- habitat
- ecology
- expand
- growth

Word list
- nutrition
- reproduction
- skeleton
- temperature
- oxygen
- respiration
- sunlight

Clues across
- 2 To get bigger, e.g. lungs when you breathe in
- 7 Group of living things living together
- 8 The bones in an animal that hold it together
- 9 Begin to grow, e.g. as a seed does in warm, damp earth
- 11 The place where a plant or animal lives
- 12 Gas found in air and which all living things use for breathing
- 14 The process of animals or plants making more of themselves

Clues down
- 1 The study of living things
- 3 Getting food and using it for growth
- 4 Natural light that allows green plants to live
- 5 How hot or cold something is
- 6 Breathing
- 10 The study of plants and animals in their environment
- 13 An animal or plant getting bigger

Alpha to Omega Activity Pack One Plus © Heinemann Educational 1997

Words you need to know 12: Chemistry

Mix and match

▶ Learn the meanings of the words below. Then cut them up, mix them up and match them up again.

Word	Meaning
atmosphere	the air around the earth
boiling point	the temperature at which a liquid changes into a gas
chemistry	the science that explains what things are made of
dissolve	to mix with a liquid to make a solution
insoluble	will not dissolve in water
melt	change from solid to liquid by using heat
metal	shiny element that will conduct electricity
oxygen	a gas found in the air – needed for burning
soluble	will dissolve in water
solution	a smooth liquid mixture

© Heinemann Educational 1997

Alpha to Omega Activity Pack One Plus

108 Words you need to know 13: Chemistry

Crossword puzzle

Word list
atmosphere   boiling point
chemistry   dissolve
insoluble

Word list
melt   metal
oxygen   soluble
solution

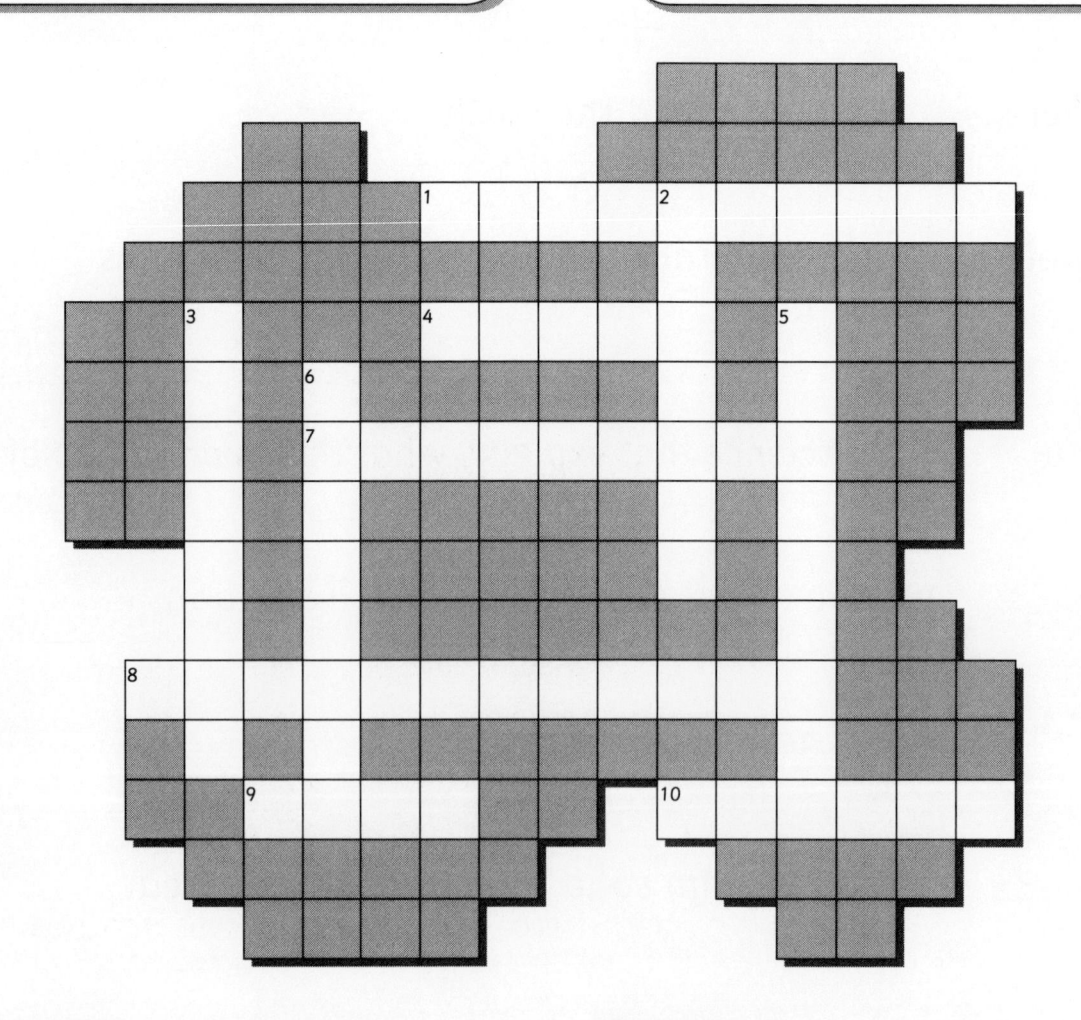

Clues across
1. The air around the earth
4. Shiny element that will conduct electricity
7. Will not dissolve in water
8. The temperature at which liquid changes into a gas
9. Change from solid to liquid by using heat
10. A gas found in the air – needed for burning

Clues down
2. Will dissolve in water
3. A smooth liquid mixture
5. The science that explains what things are made of
6. To mix with a liquid to make a solution

Alpha to Omega Activity Pack One Plus   © Heinemann Educational 1997

Words you need to know 14: Physics

Mix and match

▶ Learn the meanings of the words below. Then cut them up, mix them up and match them up again.

Word	Meaning
electricity	a kind of energy – made or occurring naturally, such as lightning
energy	this has many forms, e.g. heat, movement, light and sound
force	what is needed to move an object
galaxy	huge cluster of stars
gravity	the force that pulls things down to the ground
reflect	to throw back light from a surface, such as a mirror
refract	to change the course of a light beam
weight	how heavy something is

110 Words you need to know 15: Physics

Crossword puzzle

Word list
- electricity
- energy
- reflect
- refract
- weight

Clues across
1. To throw back light from a surface, such as a mirror
3. To change the course of a light beam
4. This has many forms, e.g. heat, movement, light and sound
5. How heavy something is

Clues down
2. A kind of energy – made or occurring naturally, such as lightning

Alpha to Omega Activity Pack One Plus © Heinemann Educational 1997